The Floral ᶓ
The Great Masters

Elizabeth Haig

Alpha Editions

This edition published in 2020

ISBN: 9789354185199 (Hardback)

ISBN: 9789354188374 (Paperback)

Design and Setting By
Alpha Editions
www.alphaedis.com
email - alphaedis@gmail.com

PREFACE

THIS little book has been written for the pleasure of those amateurs who are more interested in the idea which inspires a picture than in the picture's workmanship. Naturally, the more accomplished the artist, the more clearly and attractively is he able to set forth his meaning; but with art criticism this book has nothing to do, and the attributions are, for the most part, simply those of the official catalogues of the respective galleries.

To explain completely even so small a branch of Christian symbolism as that of flowers, an exhaustive knowledge is required of the development of Christian theology, and of the varying force with which different doctrines appealed at different times to the public mind. But still, these notes may be of some interest to those who care to trace in the work sanctioned by the Church and reverenced by the people the history of Western idealism, and who are sometimes puzzled by the conventions employed by the Masters to illustrate the Divine Mysteries.

CONTENTS

v

CONTENTS

LIST OF ILLUSTRATIONS

THE FLORAL SYMBOLISM
OF THE GREAT MASTERS

I

EMBLEMS AND SYMBOLS[1]

SINCE the earliest days of Christianity the Church has made use of emblems. The Early Church used them partly protectively to conceal their faith from the pagans, and partly because it lacked artists capable of worthily depicting the Godhead in human form. Even when the days of persecution had passed, the Church, restrained by reverential tradition, by

[1] Dr March states very clearly the difference between a symbol and an emblem. 'A symbol stands for an abstract idea, an emblem denotes a concrete thing, an attribute appears in apposition with the person it qualifies; for example, in a presentment of the Blessed Virgin, the lily that she holds in her hand or that flowers by her side is her attribute. When the lily appears alone it represents the Queen of Heaven and is her emblem, but if it indicates purity it is a symbol.'

poverty perhaps, and perhaps by the Eastern fear of the 'graven image,' continued to represent Christ as the True Vine and the Apostles as sheep or as doves.

But at the beginning of the fourth century the Emperor Constantine established Christianity as the religion of the state. New, and often magnificent, churches were built in each town and the Emperor placed in the hands of the ecclesiastics a large portion of the royal revenues.

In these grand new basilicas the simple decoration of the Catacombs and tiny ancient chapels was not sufficient. The ample walls offered a splendid field for the mosaicist and Byzantine taste demanded elaborate pictorial effects. Representations of the Redeemer appeared surrounded by the Apostles, the prophets and the four-and-twenty elders of Revelation. Saints and martyrs were introduced, and later we find imperial personages, Justinian surrounded by his guards and Theodora followed by the ladies of her court. It became necessary to distinguish the figures one from another and therefore symbolism was largely introduced.

The Deity was placed within the *mandorla*, symbol of perfect blessedness. The prophets were awarded broken wheels to denote their imperfect revelation, and the apostles books, to signify their fuller knowledge. Haloes were carefully differentiated. Virgin saints carried palms or laurel crowns, and martyrs had the instruments of their martyrdom placed beside them. Some figures carried scrolls on which were inscribed texts which gave the clue to their identity, others simply had their names written above their heads, but both these latter devices were useless to the ignorant.

At the Renaissance, when art had a fuller life and wider aims, it was not sufficient to thus merely label the persons represented. The traditions of Byzantine art once broken, the painter was free to set upon the panel all the beauty that his mind could conceive and that his hand could execute. He had no longer to paint a Christ or a Madonna correct to a formula, but none the less he was bound to depict figures which should be instantly recognizable as God incarnate and the meek Mother of Christ. So from his freedom sprang the problem which has occupied the religious painter ever since, the painting of a soul's quality, the making visible to the world of the beauty of holiness.

During the great century of art, achievement came. Raphael, Leonardo, Michael Angelo, Perugino required and used no symbol to express the majesty of Christ or the purity of the Virgin Mother. They had that power to make visible the intangible which, in art, is genius. But among the earlier artists of the thirteenth and fourteenth centuries, he who was unable to show by the announcing angel's attitude and mien that his message was one of peace and goodwill, placed a branch of olive in his hand, and he who despaired of adequately depicting the immaculate purity of the Virgin, emphasized his point by setting a pot of spotless lilies by her side. So was the intention of the least-accomplished of artists made clear, even to the unlettered.

After the first effervescence of the Renaissance had died down, the laws of sacred art became once more fixed, though never again (except in Spain beneath the Inquisition) with the strictness of the Byzantine school. Art as a teacher of religion required to be as conservative as the Catholic Church with which it was allied, and the symbolism of the fourteenth century has remained with few additions or modifications to our own day. When devotional pictures multiplied, emblems passed into what may be termed the heraldry of the Church. Though also used in decoration, their primary use upon altar vessels and Church furniture was to distinguish the object as sacred, or as the property of the Church, in the same way as the royal arms or a private crest indicated the ownership of secular things. They appeared on the banners used in processions of the Church and on the badges and insignia of religious orders, but were very seldom used in pictorial art. Indeed, it is in the early Flemish school alone that pictures similar to the van Eycks' ' Adoration of the Mystic Lamb ' [1] or to their ' Fountain of Life ' [2] are found, where angels, prophets, saints and patriarchs bow down before the emblem, not the figure, of the Saviour.

During the first twelve centuries of Christi-

[1] Ghent Cathedral.   [2] The Prado, Madrid.

anity the emblems and symbols of the Church were drawn from many sources; those that were introduced at the Renaissance were fruits and flowers. The Christ-Child holds the apple, symbol of the Fall, or a pomegranate showing the seeds, symbol of the Church. The lily typifies the spotless purity of the Virgin. Saint Dorothea is crowned with roses; Saint Joseph holds the flowering rod. There were, of course, other symbols used. Allegorical figures held the sword of justice or the scales of judgment; the mandorla, the halo, the orb of sovereignty and the book of knowledge survived from the Byzantine school; but those symbols which first appeared or came into fashion, as it were, at the Renaissance were fruits and flowers.

It was not strange that it should be so. The new interest in the literature of ancient Greece and Rome had revived the old classical love of nature, of running brooks and leafy forests, and of all the fresh unspoiled things which shoot up clean and fragrant from the earth. Saint Francis with his ' jesters of the Lord ' had gone singing through the vineyards praising God for the light of the sun, for the birds, for the grass. His song was taken up by the troubadours, who also sang of the fair things of the fields, though their *leit motif* was earthly, rather than heavenly, love.

The minnesingers of Germany sang of roses, spring-tide, love and chivalry, and three of the sweetest-throated, Walther von der Vogelweide, Godfried von Strassburg and Conrad von Würtzburg, each before he died, composed a song in honour of the Virgin.

In Provence the Lady Clémence Isaure instituted the *Jeux Floraux*, and for those who excelled in song there were three awards, a violet, an eglantine and a marigold, all wrought in gold. Later a silver lily was added as the prize for the best sonnet celebrating the perfections of the Virgin. The rules of this May-day tournament of song proclaimed that 'these games are for the amusement of the people, for the honour of God as the giver of good gifts of trees and flowers, and to praise Him, because nature, which had been dead, now lives again.'

The world was now beginning to see the value of these 'good gifts.' Chaucer could find no higher emblem for the Virgin than a flower:

' And thou that art the floure of Virgins all; '

while Dante, who, more than any other single writer, has influenced sacred art, uses the same imagery:

' Here is the Rose
Wherein the Word Divine was made incarnate,
And here the lilies, by whose order known
The way of life was followed.'

The Churchmen of the day caught the spirit of the Humanists, and there sprang up a school of symbolists who concerned themselves largely with plants, fruits and flowers. The writings of the early symbolists, Origen, Saint Melitus, Bishop of Sardes, Saint Jerome, Saint Ambrose, Walafrid Strabo and Raban Maur, Archbishop of Mayence, were re-studied and their allusions to the plant world noted. Durandus, Bishop of Mende, whose *Rationale*, published in 1295, is still considered the supreme authority on the spiritual significance of Church architecture and Church ornament, held flowers in general to be the emblems of goodness. 'They repre-

sent, like the trees, those good works which
have the virtues for roots.' Growing things,
he considered, could very beautifully supple-
ment the ritual of the Church, and he recom-
mends that ' on Palm Sunday the people should
deck themselves with flowers, olive branches
and palms, the flowers to signify the virtués of
the Holy One, the olive branches His office as
peace-bringer and the palms His victory over
Satan.'

There were those symbolists who, like
Durandus of Mende and the Cardinal Petrus
of Capua, valued the symbol entirely as a means
of interpreting the doctrines of the Church.
Their definition was that of Hugues de Saint-
Victor: ' The symbol is the allegorical representation of a Christian principle under a material form '; and they simply searched for those
objects which best suited their purpose. Then
there were those symbolists who, like Saint
Hildegarde, Abbess of Rupertsburg, mixed their
symbolism strangely with herbalism and magic.
A plant of healing virtues was a good plant,
attributed to the Virgin or a saint, and typifying their virtues, and a harmful plant was evil,

B

beneath the patronage of the Devil, typifying and inducing envy, hatred, or perhaps
malice.

Lastly there were the mystic symbolists, and
it is they who have had most influence on
pictorial art. There were those who, like Saint
Bernard of Clairvaux, could discern through
the darkened glass of Old Testament metaphor the divine facts of New Testament revelation, and those who, like Saint Mectilda of
Germany, were favoured by Heaven with clear
and detailed visions, in which Christ Himself
deigned to explain the complicated symbolism
of His surroundings, His embroidered robes
and jewelled ornaments. And there were those
mystics who were not in holy orders, who did
not claim direct communication with Heaven,
yet who have, nevertheless, by giving shape
and colour to the vague indications of Holy
Writ as to the future state, and by material-
izing, as it were, the illusive inner vision of
things invisible, profoundly influenced the religious sentiment, if not the theology, of the
world. Chief among them is the poet Dante,
the friend of Giotto and the spiritual father

of both the poets and the artists of the Italian
Renaissance. In Germany his place was taken
by Conrad von Würtzburg, a poet of infinitely
less genius but who equally influenced his native
art, at least as far as devotional representations
of the Virgin Mary were concerned. He was
a minnesinger who consecrated the last effort
of a long life to praising the virtues of her whom
he terms 'The Empress of Heaven.' About
the year 1286 he wrote 'The Golden Forge,'
which he describes as:

> ' A golden song
> Forged in the smithy of my heart
> And beautifully inlaid
> With the jewelled thoughts of my heart.'

It is an eulogy of the Virgin, close-packed with
allegory, simile and metaphor, which are borrowed
for the greater part from the Fathers of the
Church, but some few are of his own finding.

His work was never to be compared with
that of the great Italian, but it very strongly
influenced the hymnology and the pictorial
expression of the cult of the Virgin in both the
Netherlands and Germany.

In England there was no great symbolist

among the early poets. They were plain tales of love and war that Chaucer told in 'English undefyled.' But the Church in England produced some beautiful mystical hymns, notably the one to the Virgin, written, perhaps, about 1350, which begins:

> 'Of a rose, a lovely rose,
> Of a rose is al myn song.'

.   .   .   .

Religious pictures are of two types: the historical, which aims at depicting a sacred scene exactly as it did occur; and the devotional, which presents a divine or holy figure in the attitude and with the surroundings best calculated to inflame the devotion of the worshipper.

To the first category belongs Rubens' 'Descent from the Cross.'[1] The dead Figure, the sustained effort of the men who detach it from the Cross, the grief-stricken women, are all depicted with perfect realism and strict attention to historical detail. It merely depicts the scene as it might have occurred, and no attempt is made to guide or suggest the emotions of the beholder.

[1] Antwerp Cathedral.

To the second category belong many of the early Crucifixions. The figure of the Saviour is emaciated to a painful degree. On each side of the Cross hover angels catching in a chalice the holy blood as it falls. At the summit a nesting pelican tears its breast; at the foot a skull is placed within a niche. Here a distinct emotional appeal is made—to man's pity, for the sufferings of the Christ; to his gratitude, since the preciousness of the holy blood is so emphasized. The pelican in its piety is the symbol of Christ's devotion to His Church, and the skull invites meditation upon the eternal death from which He saved us.

In pictures of the devotional type the spiritual cause or effect of the incident illustrated is usually indicated by symbols. The reason why the Godhead sits as a child upon His Mother's knee is indicated by the apple which He holds in His hand. As the fruit of the Tree of Knowledge of Good and Evil it is the symbol of Adam's fault, which, through His incarnation, Christ repaired—and, thereby, to instructed Christians, it foretells the tragedy of the Crucifixion. So, in an Annunciation, the lily in the angel Gabriel's hand indicates the quality by which Mary found favour in God's sight, and it foreshadows also the sinless birth of the Saviour.

It should be clearly understood to which figure in a composition the symbols used refer. When a personage of mortal birth, prophet, apostle, martyr or saint, holds a symbol or attribute, it almost invariably refers to his own history. Archangels usually hold their own attribute, but the symbols or emblems which angels carry, or which are used decoratively, placed against the sky or laid upon the ground, are always to be referred to the principal figure in the scene represented. The sword and lily in a ' Last Judgment ' represent the omnipotence and integrity of the Judge; the rose and lily in an ' Assumption ' the love and the purity of the Madonna; the palm in a martyrdom the triumph of the martyr.

II

THE FLOWER SYMBOLISTS

CHRISTIAN symbolists divided the plant world into three divisions—the good, the bad, and those which, from want of definite characteristics, were not worthy of notice. In their judgment they were guided by several principles.

In the first place, and this was the most important method, they searched the Scriptures for their warrant as to the good or evil tendencies of any plant or flower. Those with whom the Divinity had identified Himself took precedence of all others. Christ had said, ' I am the True Vine,' and the vine, since the earliest days of Christianity, has had the place of highest honour in the decoration of Christian churches as the emblem of Christ Himself. When the difficulties were removed which prevented the Early Church from representing Christ under His own form, the emblem was less seen, but it has always remained a sacred plant, and

23

designs based upon its form still frequently decorate the altar and the sacred vessels.

Also those plants introduced as metaphors in the Song of Solomon, ' the flower of the field,' ' the lily of the valleys,' ' the lily among thorns,' ' the orchard of pomegranates,' myrrh and camphire, spikenard, saffron and cinnamon, trees of frankincense and ' the chief spices,' which refer to the ' Beloved ' and the ' Spouse,' are all considered holy plants, and by the Roman Catholic Church are assigned to the Virgin Mary.

In the beautiful twenty-fourth chapter of Ecclesiasticus, too, Christian symbolists have recognized the Virgin Mary beneath the figure of Wisdom, and hold as sanctified those growing things to which she is likened.

' I was exalted like a palm tree in Engeddi, and as a rose plant in Jericho, as a fair olive tree in a pleasant field, and grew up as a plane tree by the water.

' As the turpentine tree I stretched out my branches, and my branches are the branches of honour and grace.

' As the vine brought I forth pleasant savour,

and my flowers are the fruit of honour and riches.'

In the second place, those flowers and plants which are beneficial to man, as the wheat and the olive, were decided to be good, and those that were hurtful to man, as the tare and the thistle, were evil. Here herbalism and magic step very close to symbolism, for healing plants, or those which were useful as a charm against the devil, were good; those which were poisonous, or used for evil purpose, such as raising a spirit, were bad. Thus the nettle, which, when used with due ceremony, dissipates fear, becomes a symbol of courage, and myrrh, which is an antidote to love-philtres and drives away voluptuous thoughts, is held to be a plant of chastity. Of this particular species of symbolism Albertus Magnus,[1] Master of Saint Thomas Aquinas, and Saint Hildegarde,[2] Abbess of Rupertsburg, were the principal exponents.

Also a plant's habit of growth was taken as an indication of its character. The cedar,

---

[1] Author of *Liber aggregationis, seu Liber mirabilium de virtutibus herbarum, lapidum et animalium.*

[2] Authoress of *The Garden of Health.*

with unbending head and grandly-spreading branches, was considered, both by Saint Melitus and Petrus of Capua, to typify pride, while the violet, wearing the colour of mourning, and keeping timidly beneath its leaves, they chose as a symbol of humility.

Some symbols were of pagan origin, for the palm of victory and the olive branch of peace were borrowed from the Romans, who had themselves inherited them from older civilizations. Their significance was not changed but simply limited and sanctified; the victory, for Christians, was the victory over sin, and the peace, the peace of God.

These various methods of determining the value of different plants as symbols did not always accord. M. Huysman, in *La Cathédrale*, a very complete study in Christian symbolism, instances the sycamore: ' Saint Melitus proclaims that the sycamore stands for cupidity. . . Raban Maur and *L'anonyme de Clairvaux* qualify it as the unbelieving Jew; Petrus of Capua compares it to the Cross, Saint Eucher to wisdom.'

Even the sifting of the text of Scripture did not always lead to identical conclusions. ' I am the rose of Sharon' (or 'the flower of the field') 'and the lily of the valleys,' sings the lover of the Canticles, who prefigures, according to Origen, Jesus Christ. But Saint Bernard of Clairvaux found that the words veiled the personality of the Virgin Mary, and other writers consider that they refer to the Church of God upon earth.

There were, in fact, two schools of symbolists though they did not differ greatly. There were those who wrote before the eleventh century and whose influence is traced in the mosaics of Rome, Ravenna and the Baptistery of Florence, and those later ones whose authority was accepted by the painters of the Italian Renaissance and through them spread throughout the Christian world. Durandus, standing midway between the two schools of symbolism, held chiefly to the more ancient, though he also recognized the newer, usage.

But after the twelfth century the painters of Siena alone kept to the ancient meaning of the symbols; Florence and the later schools broke away entirely

As far as flower-symbols were concerned the chief difference was in the use of the lily, which from being the flower indicative of heavenly bliss became the especial flower of the Virgin, typifying her purity. Also the rose, the flower of martyrdom, became the symbol of divine love, and the palm tree and the acanthus dropped out of devotional representations altogether.

In the main, after the twelfth century, symbolists were agreed. There were certain fruits and flowers about which there never had been any doubt. The vine had been the emblem of Jesus Christ from the beginning of Christian theology. The white lily, as a symbol of chastity, came perhaps from the Hebrews, but all Christian writers were agreed as to its fitness as a symbol of purity and as an emblem or attribute of the Virgin Mary. The violet was the symbol of humility, and therefore, say Petrus of Capua and Saint Mectilda, the emblem of Christ when on earth. Saint Mectilda and Bishop Durandus, for the same reason, consider it the emblem of confessors.

The rose was long in disgrace as the flower of Venus. But even saints could not exclude it from their lives, and gradually it crept into

Christian hagiology. Roses decorate some of the most poetical of the histories in the *Legenda Aurea*, which was compiled by Jacobus de Voragine, Archbishop of Genoa, during the last half of the thirteenth century, and there are roses in plenty in the pictures of the fifteenth century. Their meaning, at first sight, is not so clearly defined as is that of some other flowers. Raban Maur and *L'anonyme de Clairvaux* had used them as the type of charity; Durandus had explained them, red and white, as emblems of martyrs and virgins. Walafrid Strabo also considered them the symbols of martyrdom, but in the Golden Legend and in the pictures of the Renaissance, when plucked and falling, or when sent from Heaven, they are symbols of divine love; when they are woven into wreaths they symbolize heavenly joy.

The symbolism of the lesser flowers is not so clear, but the water lily and the saffron as well as the rose were held by Raban Maur to be symbols of charity; verdure, according to Durandus, was the emblem of beginners in the faith; the heath, hyssop, convolvulus and violet all represent humility; the lettuce temperance; the elder, zeal; and the thyme, activity. Of these, however, with the exception of the violet, Christian art has taken little note.

There are certain flowers which appear repeatedly in pictures which represent the garden of Heaven; they grow in the ' Enclosed Garden ' of the Madonna, and surround the Infant Christ when He is laid upon the ground to receive adoration. They are the rose and the lily, and also the violet, the pink and the strawberry, the last with fruit and flowers together. The symbolists are unanimous in ascribing humility to the violet; the pink or carnation, which is usually introduced when there are no roses, is, like the rose, the flower of divine love; the strawberry with fruit and flower represents the good works of the righteous, or the fruits of the spirit.

To these are sometimes added the clover and the columbine. According to the legend, Saint Patrick was the first to use the trefoil as an illustration of the Trinity in Unity, and the shamrock or clover is the emblem of the Holy Trinity. The little doves which make up the flower of the columbine wonderfully resemble

the little doves which in early art, particularly
in the French miniatures of the thirteenth and
fourteenth centuries, represent the seven gifts
of the Holy Spirit. It is true that in the columbine the little doves number five, not seven,
but the Flemish artists, always extremely careful
in their symbolism, rectified this by painting
the plant with seven blooms upon it. It should
only be used as the attribute of God the Son.

Towards the end of the fifteenth century a
tiny niche was made for the daisy in Christian
iconography. It is found almost exclusively
in ' Adorations,' where it replaces the *lilium
candidum*. It was felt that, suitable as the
tall austere lily might be to express the Virgin's
purity or the celibacy of the monastic saints,
the little wide-eyed daisy was a prettier, sweeter
symbol of the perfect innocence of the Divine
Child.

The jasmine is not strictly a holy flower and
has been neglected by the writers on symbolism,
but it appears repeatedly in religious art. Its
star-shaped blossom seems to be the symbol
of divine hope or of heavenly felicity, and it is
found with roses and lilies beside the Madonna.

It forms the crowns of angels, of saints, and of the Madonna herself. When it is the attribute of the Infant Christ it recalls the Heaven from which He came.

The English and Flemish miniaturists add to these the pansy, which is the old herb Trinity,[1] bearing the same meaning as the clover.

In the Netherlands and Germany the lily of the valley was also used, with meek purity as its significance.

All these flowers, on account of some accident of shape, colour or habit of growth, were considered holy flowers, while others, such as the buttercup, the narcissus, the forget-me-not, were rejected as meaningless. Fruit in general represents good works, or the fruits of the Spirit, faith, hope and peace, and is accounted good; the vine is the emblem of Christ Himself, but the fruit, usually taken to be the apple,

[1] 'This is that herb which such physicians as are licensed to blaspheme by authority without danger of having their tongues burned through with a hot iron called an herb of the Trinity; it is also called, by those who are more moderate, three faces in a hood . . . and in Sussex we call them pancies.' Culpeper's *Herbal.*

which grew on the Tree of Knowledge of Good and Evil, is an accursed thing.

There are flowers, too, which are the flowers of evil. The poppy is the emblem of sloth and also dedicated to Venus; the tulip is beloved of necromancers; the black hellebore and the mandrake are used by witches in their spells, though, strangely enough, Conrad von Würtzburg compares the Virgin Mary to the ' healing mandrake root.' Also the nettle is the symbol of envy, the hellebore of scandal, and the cyclamen of voluptuousness, for, according to Theophrastus, it was used in the composition of love philtres.

As to thorns and briars, Saint Thomas Aquinas and Saint Anselm are agreed that thorn branches signify the minor sins, and briars (or thistles) those major ones ' *quae pungunt conscientiam propriam,*' etc.

Above all the buckthorn is blamed, for of its branches, says Rohault de Fleury, was formed the Crown of Thorns.

In art, however, the flowers of evil scarcely appear. The rose is still sometimes the flower of Venus and symbolizes the pomps and vanities

c

of the world, and there are the thorns of sin and death. Some of the early Flemish and German artists painted certain bitter herbs, notably the dandelion, in scenes from the Passion, but Christian iconography has concerned itself chiefly with those plants and flowers which, with the approval of theologians, represent the attributes of the Divinity, of the Virgin Mary and of angels, saints and prophets.

It may be noticed that while the sacred flowers are not unfrequently introduced into profane scenes, the non-sacred flowers, for instance the daffodils and foxgloves of the hunting scenes on old Flemish tapestry, are never introduced as symbols, and rarely as details, in devotional subjects.

The same symbolism holds good within the whole Western Church, and those Reformed Churches which have rejected painted and carved images have preserved a good many of the older symbols in the details of church decoration. The most important symbols of Christianity, the Lamb, the Dove, the Cross, the Glory, the Halo, remain always unchanged. It is the lesser, and more especially the flower symbols, which vary in different countries and different schools of painting. Italy being the headquarters of the Church, and also the centre from which pictorial art spread over Europe, most symbols are of Latin origin; but they were modified and often amplified by inherited tradition, climate and the general trend of the national religious sentiment. So in Italian art, after its re-birth, we find a love of simple lines, of refined types, of flowers, and a striving at first unconscious, then definite, after classical ideals, while the Northern nations, less happy in their traditions, never quite conquered their love of barbaric splendour; a rose wrought in pure gold was to them more truly a symbol of divine love than a fresh rose of the field.

The most important factor in the modification of flower symbolism was climate. As the primary use of a symbol was to instruct the unlearned, the symbol which was to interpret the hidden mystery must be a familiar object. A rare or exotic plant would rather have complicated than simplified the teaching. So we find the pomegranate and the olive in Italian pictures, but not in those of the Netherlands; the columbine and the lily of the valley in German, but not in Spanish art.

But it was not climate alone that determined the use or disuse of any particular plant as a symbol. If the fleur-de-lys, founded upon the iris form, had not been borne by the House of Burgundy, which protected the early Flemish school, it is possible that the iris might not have appeared in the early Flemish pictures as a flower of the Virgin, and certainly had there not been a continual interchange of Flemish merchandise, which included painted panels, for Spanish gold, the iris would not have taken its place as the characteristic flower of a Spanish 'Immaculate Conception.'

Also, had there not been ceaseless warfare and everlasting hatred between Florence and Siena, it is possible that Siena would have adopted the lily as an attribute of Mary in an Annunciation instead of using invariably the olive branch. But the lily was the badge of Florence and the cities were desperately jealous of each other, both in painting and in politics, and this seems to be the real reason of the conservatism of Sienese art.

On the whole the symbolism of the Netherlands is the most careful and just, and each flower was painted also with such exquisite minuteness that there is no possibility of mistaking the variety. Italian symbolism was always apt to be superficial, and after the fifteenth century often became confused with decoration. Also the Italians painted flowers carelessly, and the lesser kinds, those in the foreground of an Adoration, for instance, are frequently impossible to identify. In Germany symbolism is at times extravagant and far-fetched though always interesting. In Spain it is poor and almost entirely borrowed. A modern writer [1] observes of Spanish art that it is material, brutal, Roman, having, from its geographical position, escaped the idealism of Greek or the mysticism of Celtic influences; and the same cause may also explain the prosaicness of its symbolism.

The English love of flowers, very noticeable in early verse, found pictorial expression chiefly in the work of the miniaturists and in the ' flower work ' details of architecture. The miniatures executed by monks usually pay attention to the symbolical value of each blossom, but the carved

[1] C. Marriott.

stone flowers common in both French and English Gothic churches were more often simply those which the fancy of the architect or the stone-cutter dictated and only represent vaguely ' good works springing from the root of virtues.'

The happiest blooming time of these symbolical flowers was the fifteenth century. In the fourteenth century artists, still timid of innovations, had limited themselves to the lily and the rose. But with increasing skill they made a wider choice, though always under the eye and with the assistance of those learned in such matters, for the majority of sacred pictures were commissioned directly by the Church or were ordered as a gift to be presented to some religious community.

There were occasionally independent spirits who, in some favourite blossom, so far unnoticed, found beauty and symbolic fitness. Thus Sano di Pietro of Siena constantly paints the bright blue cornflower (which in Italy shares its name of *fiordaliso* with the iris, the lily and the heraldic fleur-de-lys) upon the heads of both angels and saints, meaning, perhaps, by the blue stars, to indicate that these beings were denizens of the heavenly spaces. However, as a rule, artists were conservative and glad to use the recognized symbols as a means of emphasizing and elucidating the sacred subject which they depicted.

But even before the end of the fifteenth century flowers began to be used for their own sake and not for their hidden meaning. Leonardo da Vinci and Albert Dürer painted just what flower or weed they chose, simply for its form or colour. In the sixteenth century flowers were often used merely as decoration, and later, with the exception of the rose, the lily, the olive branch and the palm, they lost all meaning. Carlo Maratta in the seventeenth century painted a figure of the Virgin[1] encircled by a heavy wreath of every sort of flower—daffodils, gentians, anemones, tulips, edelweiss, roses and lilies, all mixed together.

In England, about the middle of the nineteenth century, there was a revival of interest in mystical and symbolical art. The Pre-raphaelite Brotherhood was formed in 1848, whose object was to bring back to modern art

[1] Corsini Gallery, Florence.

the sincerity and earnestness of those painters who had preceded Raphael. The originator of the movement, Dante Gabriel Rossetti, adopted in his early work not only the simplicity of type and the exceedingly careful finish of the primitives, but borrowed also their system of symbolism. His followers, however, and in particular Holman Hunt, broke away from the old traditions of religious art, painting allegorical subjects suggested by Christ's parables and sayings rather than the scenes of His birth and Passion on which the dogmas of the Church were founded, and with the traditional subjects they left aside also the traditional symbols.

The greatest of modern English mystical painters, George Frederick Watts, uses flowers as details, and apparently as symbols. But their exact meanings are obscure and apparently not those attributed to them by the great masters of past centuries.

THE BADGE OF THE ORDER OF THE LILY OF NAVARRE

THE FLOWERS OF HEAVEN
Mosaic of the 13th century
(Baptistry, Florence)

To face page 41]

III

THE LILY

GIOACCHINO DI FIORE, the mystical theologian
who founded the community of ' The Flower,'
and who is held by some to be the spiritual
father of Saint Francis, writing in the last decade
of the twelfth century, divided the life of humanity into three periods. In the first, during the
reign of the Father, men lived under the rule of
the law; in the second, reigned over by the
Son, men live beneath the rule of grace; in
the third the Spirit shall reign and men shall
live in the plenitude of love. The first saw
the shining of the stars; the second sees the
whitening of the dawn; the third will behold the
glory of the day. The first produced nettles;
the second gives roses; the third will be the
age of lilies.

Thus as daylight to dawn or starlight, and as
love to grace and fear, were lilies to every other
flower or weed, and since the twelfth century, in

Christian art, lilies have had precedence of every other growing thing.

The earliest use of the lily by the artists of the Christian Church was to indicate the delights of Paradise. Raban Maur, Archbishop of Mayence in 847, writes of lilies as the symbols of celestial beatitude, and that is apparently what they represent in the mosaics of Rome, Ravenna and the Baptistery of Florence, where they spring from the ground in the scenes which represent Heaven.

But by the tenth century the Church had commenced to adopt the pre-Christian employment of the lily as the symbol of purity, and the rose gradually took the lily's place as the flower of heavenly bliss.

The lily of sacred art is the *lilium candidum*, sometimes called the Madonna lily, or the lily of Saint Catharine. It is said to be a native of the Levant, but appears to have spread with Roman civilization throughout Europe. The suggestion of abstract purity is arresting and direct. The stalk is straight and upright, the leaves narrow, plain, almost austere. At the top of the long stalk the flowers cluster, each chalice-shaped, and sending to the sky a perfume which is singularly sweet and piercing. Their form is simple but noble, and they are above all remarkable for the immaculate and luminous whiteness of their firm petals.

After the twelfth century the lily is always used as the symbol of purity in its perfection, and is most usually associated with the Virgin Mary and with saints of the monastic orders. More rarely it is used as an attribute of the Persons of the Holy Trinity. In a large picture [1] representing the Trinity in Glory, by an unknown Neapolitan painter of the seventeenth century, God the Father holds a stalk of lilies in his left hand, above which hovers the mystic Dove. Since Christian iconography gives no attributes to God the Father except the orb and crown of omnipotence, the lily must be taken as the attribute of the Holy Ghost ; and in a rare subject, The Adoration of the Holy Ghost,[2] ascribed by Behrenson to the *Amico di Sandro*, the two angels with swinging censers and lovely floating draperies, who adore the hovering Dove, carry each a lily. The Dove in conjunction with the lily is also found upon the great central doors of

[1] Naples Museum.   [2] Stroganoff Collection, Rome.

Saint Peter in Rome. They are of bronze, and were executed between 1439 and 1445 by Antonio Filarete. There are two panels with elaborate borders and much interesting detail. On one is Saint Peter with the keys and on the other Saint Paul. Saint Paul is of the traditional type, bald and bearded, and holds in his right hand a drawn sword. By his side is a large vase of lilies, and on the highest flower, its beak touching the sword's hilt, is the Dove, encircled by a halo. The lilies and the Dove are introduced apparently to correct the impression of violence given by the uplifted sword, the instrument of the Apostle's martyrdom, and together representing the Holy Spirit, they recall Saint Paul's own phrase, ' the sword of the Spirit.'

As an attribute of God the Son, lilies are used in those pictures known as Adorations, where the divine Child is laid upon the ground and the Mother kneels before Him in worship; and in those pictures where she holds Him, no longer a very young infant, on a ledge or pedestal before her. In these pictures all the symbolism refers to the Child, and if He lie among roses and lilies they signify respectively divine love and perfect sinlessness. If angels hold vases of lilies on either side, these lilies recall that He was born of a Virgin.

The first Adorations were painted by the Florentine masters of the fifteenth century. In an early example by Filippo Lippi [1] the flowers are small and the species scarcely to be determined. Neri di Bicci [2] painted roses and lilies, and Luca della Robbia [3] has placed the Child beneath a freely-growing clump of tall lilies. The Virgin kneels before Him, while heavenly hands hold above her head a crown ornamented with the royal fleur-de-lys. Botticelli [4] appears to have been the first to have substituted the daisy for the lily, and to the daisy he added the violet of humility, and the strawberry, which symbolized the fruits of the spirit. These flowers were constantly repeated in this connection, a comparatively late example of their use being in the Adoration of Perugino, now ir Munich.

These same flowers are found in the North,

[1] Accademia, Florence.
[2] Ex Convent of S. Apollonia, Florence.
[3] Bargello, Florence.
[4] Adoration, Pitti Palace, private apartments.

but as Northern artists preferred incidents definitely recounted by the Scriptures to more imaginative devotional subjects, they were transferred to Nativities or Adorations by the Shepherds.

In Siena during the fourteenth century, and in the school of Giotto, the lily, usually a single lily-cup, is sometimes placed in the hands of the Infant Christ. Here it is not the symbol of purity, but in accordance with the older symbolism it is the flower of Paradise. Siena was extremely conservative, and for its artists the Holy Child was still the royal Child of the Byzantine school, richly clothed, His right hand raised in blessing or holding the orb of sovereignty. Sometimes He holds a scroll, announcing His high mission, with the words ' Ego sum lux mundi ' or ' Ego sum via veritas et vita.' More stress is laid upon His divinity than upon His humanity, and there is absolutely nothing to hint at or forecast His passion. He appears simply as the bringer of peace and blessing, and in His hand is still the flower of Paradise, the same lily which grows beside His throne in the mosaics.

Gradually, however, a fruit replaced the

flower in the Christ-Child's hand. At first the fruit, following an artistic tradition as old as the fourth century, was also a promise of heavenly bliss, it was a fruit from the heavenly gardens; but it was soon identified as the fruit of the tree of Knowledge of Good and Evil, since He, as the Second Adam, had come to repair the fault of the first.

Meanwhile in Florence, during the fifteenth century, the lily, already the flower of the virgin saints, was attributed more especially to the Virgin Mary as the symbol of spotless purity, and it became accepted throughout Christendom with this significance.

Therefore, on the rare occasions after the fourteenth century when the lily is placed in the hand of the Infant Christ it is the symbol of purity, of His perfect sinlessness. In the Enthroned Madonna of Luca Signorelli [1] He holds a large stalk of *lilium candidum*. In the great majority of representations of the Madonna with the Child in her arms only the symbol in the Child's own hand refers to Him; other symbols refer to Mary. But in this picture, to

[1] Cathedral, Perugia.

the jewelled cross of the Baptist is attached a scroll with the legend, ' *Ecce Agnus Dei*,' and all the symbols are the attributes of the Saviour. Besides the lily, which denotes perfect sinlessness, there are two transparent vases in which are jasmine, violets and roses. The jasmine's starry blooms recall the Heaven which He has left, the violet is a symbol of His humility, and the rose of His divine love. In the wreath behind the throne is jasmine again, with pendant trails of white convolvulus, which is also an emblem of humility.[1]

Occasionally the Infant Christ is represented offering a branch of lilies to a Saint,[2] and then the lily represents the gift of chastity, which He bestows.

It is only in modern times that Christ, grown to manhood, has been represented with a lily in His hand. An instance is the fresco illustrating the parable of the Wise and the Foolish Virgins, painted in 1864, by Lord Leighton, P.R.A., for Lindhurst Church. The virgins stand on either side of the Celestial Bridegroom, who holds in

[1] J. K. Huysmans, *La Cathédrale*.
[2] Attributed to Giotto. Collection of A. E. Street, Esq.

His left hand the lily which emphasizes the mystical character of the divine nuptials.

It may be noticed in this connection that modern, and more particularly Protestant, ecclesiastical art takes its subjects largely from the parables of Christ, a usage unknown to the Roman Catholic Church during the period when the great masters of art were in her service.

Northern mediæval art, that is, the art of the Flemish and German schools, introduced the lily into representations of the Last Judgment, placing the sword and stalk of lilies, ray-wise, behind the head of the judging Christ. In the very early representations of this subject Christ is depicted with a two-edged sword issuing from His mouth, in illustration of the text of the Revelation of Saint John:

' And out of his mouth went a sharp two-edged sword.'

And again:

' Which sword proceeded out of his mouth.'

But pictorially it was ugly and theologically it was harsh, suggesting wrath rather than mercy as the determining impulse at the final doom. Then men remembered the promise to the righteous:

D

'The wilderness and the solitary places shall
be glad for them; and the desert shall rejoice
and blossom as the rose.'[1]

And in a copy of the *Biblia Pauperum*[2] of the
fifteenth century we find a branch of roses so
placed as to balance the sword, both set diago-
nally like rays, one on each side of the head of
Christ. The rose was placed on Christ's right
hand above the forgiven souls, and clearly
typified divine love and mercy; the sword on the
left was above the damned, and typified divine
condemnation.

But almost immediately the rose was replaced by the lily. The lily was, in the fifteenth
century, the one distinctly sacred flower. Its
lance-like habit of growth made it a most symmetrical pendant to the sword, and possibly, too,
the Church of the North, stern both in religious
sentiment and in its pictorial expression, preferred the lily, which typified the integrity of the
judging God, to the rose, symbol of His mercy.

The Netherlands adopted the symbol. It
appears in Memling's most impressive Last

[1] Isaiah xxxv. 1.
[2] Wolfenbüttel Copy, Bibliothèque Nationale.

Judgment,[1] and in the Last Judgment of Lucas van Leyden.[2] The same device was used by Albert Dürer[3] and many of the less known German masters; but Rubens, in his magnificent picture now in Munich, has replaced the lily by a sceptre.

The lily, used in this connection, is not found in Italian art, for though the Netherlands, Germany and England adopted the symbolism of Italy, Italy, though admiring greatly the technical excellence of the Flemish, rarely assimilated the Northern conventions for the expression of the intangible.

But the lily is usually reserved for virgin saints and martyrs, and more particularly for her whom Chaucer names

'Floure of Virgins all'

—that is, the Virgin Mary.

The Venerable Bede, writing in the early part of the eighth century, declares 'the great white lily' to be a fit emblem of the resurrection of the Virgin ; the pure white petals signifying her

[1] Marienpfarrkirchen, Danzig.
[2] Town Museum, Leyden.
[3] 'The Smaller Passion,' British Museum.

body; the golden anthers her soul within, shining with celestial light.

According to Petrus Cantius, cantor of the Cathedral School of Paris in the early part of the thirteenth century, the lily represented the daughter of Joachim herself, by reason of its whiteness, its aroma, delectable above all others, its curative virtues, and finally because it springs from uncultivated soil as the Virgin was the issue of Jewish parents.

As to its curative virtues, it may be added that an anonymous English monk, writing in the thirteenth century, prescribes the lily as a sovereign remedy for burns; and for the reason that ' it is a figure of the Madonna, who also cures burns, that is, the vices or burns of the soul.' [1]

But though theologians occasionally used the lily as a symbol of virginity, before the eleventh century we do not find it associated with the Mother of Christ pictorially, either as her emblem or her attribute. There are no lilies in the Catacombs, and those in the early mosaics are decorative, or symbols of the joy of Heaven.

[1] J. K. Huysmans, *La Cathédrale.*

The miniaturists occasionally used the flower as the attribute of virgin martyrs, but not in representations of the Virgin.

It was by a Spanish king that the lily was first definitely, and in a manner pictorially, associated with the Mother of Christ—as her own flower. In the eleventh century Spaniards and Moors were each fighting for their faith, and the Moslems instituted military orders called *rábitos*, the members of which were vowed to perpetual warfare against the ' infidel.'

The Christian knights were not to be outdone, and in 1043 Garcias of Navarre founded an order of chivalry vowed to the service of the Virgin, which he named ' the Order of the Lily of Navarre.'

Edmondson ' writes: ' The Order of " Our Lady of the Lily," or " of Navarre," was instituted in the city of Nagera by Garcias, the sixth King of Navarre, in the year 1043, on the occasion of a miraculous image of the Virgin Mary issuing forth of a lily, and holding the Infant Jesus in her arms, being then discovered in that city. This order was composed of thirty

' *Complete Book of Heraldry*, 1780. vol. i.

knights, chosen out of the principal ancient
families in Navarre, Biscay and old Castile.
Each of these knights wore on his breast a lily
embroidered in silver, and, on all festivals and
holy days, he wore about his neck a collar composed of a double chain of gold interlaced with
Gothic capital letters 𝔐𝔐 ; and pendent there-
unto an oval medal, whereon was enamelled,
on a white ground, a lily of gold springing out of
a mount, supporting a Gothic capital letter 𝔐𝔐,
ducally crowned.' [1]

Thus the lily became the gage of the Virgin
borne by her knights. She was now gradually
moving from the subordinate though glorious
station as Mother of the Incarnate Word to a
position of her own as Queen of Heaven. Saint
Ferdinand, possibly unwilling to confront the
Moslem with the Christ whom they themselves
revered as a prophet, bore upon his saddle-bow
the ivory *Virgen de las Batallas*,[2] and perhaps

[1] 'The effigies of the Kings of Navarre, successors to Garcias,
are still to be seen with this order about their necks in the Church
of St Mary at Nagera, St Saviour's de Layra and St Mary la
Reale of Pompelona, as also in the church at Ronceneux, and
at St John's de la Pigna.' (Edmondson.)
[2] Now in Seville Cathedral.

what specially endeared her to the people of Spain was the knowledge that in the fealty they paid her the infidel could have neither part nor lot. The chosen knight of the Immaculate Virgin was, of course, *Santiago*, Saint James, the patron saint of Spain, but every Spanish cavalier acknowledged himself the servitor of the Lady of the Lily.

Rather more than fifty years after the founding of the Order of the Lily of Navarre the poet-saint, Bernard of Clairvaux, was preaching his famous series of Homilies on the Song of Solomon. The sermons were eighty in number, each based on the text of the Canticles, and each celebrating the perfections of the Virgin. Differing from Origen, he found the Virgin Mary, not the Christ, to be the speaker of the words: ' I am the rose of Sharon and the lily of the valleys.' Differing again from the Church father, he further identified ' the lily among thorns,' she who is addressed as ' my sister, my spouse,' with the Virgin and not with the Church of God upon Earth.

Saint Bernard was the most popular preacher of his time ; his sermons became known through-

out the Christian world, and to his influence may
be traced the high position which the Mother
of Christ now holds in the Roman Catholic
Church. But, so far, the lily had not appeared
in pictorial art in connection with the Virgin.

In the twelfth century, however, we find
ecclesiastical seals which bear the figure of the
Virgin holding by the left hand (or right, as it
would appear on the impress) the Child, and in
her right a branch of lilies. Two of these seals,
that of the Dean and Chapter of Lincoln and
that of Thornholm Priory in Lincolnshire, are
now in the British Museum. It seems to have
been the fashion in the eleventh, twelfth and
thirteenth centuries to engrave the owner's
figure on a seal with a flower in the hand. On
the seal of Capet Henri I he is shown with a
sceptre in one hand and a fleur-de-lys in the
other, and the figures on the seals of the Queens
of France have a flower in either hand. Therefore it was only natural, when cutting the Virgin's
figure on a seal, that the craftsman should give
her a flower too, and the Virgin's own flower,
the lily.

The conservatism of churchmen and the

traditions of Byzantine art still kept lilies at the threshold of the Church till the Renaissance came. It came like the spring, uncertainly at first, with puffs and gusts and relapses, but every day the atmosphere grew more genial, more life-giving, till at last every branch of human thought was alive and growing. The old early Christian fear of beauty as a devil's lure was dying fast, and as scholars and artists studied with new interest the legacies of ancient Greece and Rome, the old pagan joy of perfect form in art as in literature revived once more. A representation of the climax of the Christian tragedy could only be an awful thing, but childhood and womanhood had the right to beauty. The old Byzantine panels of the Child-Christ and His Mother were little more than a formula; the lines and colour were not beautiful, though understood to represent a thing of beauty. Now artists and people required that she who, on the word of Scripture, was 'the fairest among women,'¹ should be adequately presented, and the Church gave consent. But it was understood that the loveliness of the Virgin should be strictly the

¹ Solomon's Song v. 9.

beauty of holiness, for Saint Ambrose had
affirmed [1] that, in the Mother of God, corporeal
beauty had been, as it were, the reflection of the
beauty of the soul, and the early artists, ham-
pered by lack of technical skill and confused by
monkish ideals of asceticism, too often rendered
their Madonnas emaciated and bloodless, even
languid and fretful in expression, mistaking the
outward signs of a subdued flesh for those of a
perfected spirit.

It was at this time that Saint Dominic came
to Italy with his fiery zeal, his devotion to the
Virgin and his Spanish traditions of the flower
of Our Lady. For him, the quality which
raised her so far above all other women was her
spotlessness ; she was ' *sin pecado*,' ' *Maria
Purissima*.' Her other phases, as Mother
of the Sorrowful, Refuge of Sinners, or Consoler of the Afflicted, were to him of secondary
importance.

Already through the preaching of Saint
Francis Italian intellect had been rendered
capable of appreciating the beauty of sim-

---

[1] ' Ut ipsa corporis species simulacrum fuerit mentis.'
De Verginit, lib. ii. chap. 2.

plicity. Each artist knew that the true beauty of the Queen of Heaven was not to be expressed by jewels or wonderfully-wrought raiment, and as the words of Saint Dominic passed from mouth to mouth, the people of Italy came to understand that the most precious virtue of Christ's Mother was her purity, symbolized very fitly by the lily. The symbol, beautiful in itself, and so suggestive of the quality it represented, impressed the imagination clearly, and presently there was a bloom of pictured lilies.

The mosaicist Cavallini,[1] Duccio di Buoninsegna,[2] Giotto,[3] Simone Martini,[4] and Orcagna[5] led the way, and the Christian artists of the world have followed. The earliest lilies flowered in Rome; but Siena, Umbria, Florence, Venice, and later the Netherlands and Germany, all soon had their votaries of the mystic flower. The French ivory workers of the fourteenth century, influenced doubtless by the tradition of the seal-cutters, frequently placed flowers in the hand of

[1] S. Maria Trastevere, Rome. [2] National Gallery, London.
[3] Lower Church, Assisi. [4] Uffizi, Florence.
[5] Or San Michele, Florence.

the Madonna. These little ivory statuettes are usually very sweet in type and often exquisite in workmanship. The Child is held on the left arm, and the right hand holds a large single lily cup, a pear-like fruit, or, more generally, a natural stalk of lilies with leaves and flowers. Always when placed beside the Virgin, or in her hand, the lily is the symbol of her purity, and a lily standing alone, as does the beautiful stem in *pietra-dura* work, which decorates the little oratory of ' Our Lady of the Annunciation ' in the Church of the Santissima Annunziata of Florence, is the emblem of the Madonna herself, the ' Lilium inter Spinas.'

Modern Biblical commentators are agreed that the ' lily of the valleys ' of the Song of Solomon is not the white lily of Europe but the scarlet anemone. The *lilium candidum* appears never to have grown in Syria. In the late spring and early summer, however, the anemones grow thickly in every grassy patch around Jerusalem and throughout Palestine. That the flower mentioned is red seems indicated by the comparison between it and the lips of the ' Beloved,' and the anemone, which responds so readily to the sun, throwing back its scarlet petals and baring its heart to the warmth, might well stand for the passionate lover of the Canticles.

But the fathers of the Church held the flower to be a *lilium*, and for the Church and for sacred art it was and remains the *lilium candidum*.

From French MS. of 14th Century

IV

THE IRIS

THE only rival to the *lilium candidum* as the lily of the Virgin is the iris. Strictly speaking, it is not a lily at all, for the *Iridacea* and the *Liliacea* are distinct botanical orders. But in Germany it is known as the sword-lily, from its sword-shaped leaves; in France it has always been identified with the 'fleur-de-lys'; in Spain it is a 'lirio' —a lily—and Shakespeare writes:

> '. . . And lilies of all kinds
> The Flower-de-luce being one.'

Its first appearance as a religious symbol is in the work of the early Flemish masters, where it both accompanies and replaces the white lily as the flower of the Virgin. Roger van der Weyden [1] paints both flowers in a vase before the Virgin, and the iris alone in another picture [2] of Mary with the Holy Child. In his ' Annunciation ' [3] the vase

[1] Frankfort-on-the-Maine.   [2] Berlin.
[3] Alte Pinakothek, Munich.

holds only white lilies. There is iris growing among the roses in Jan van Eyck's ' Virgin of the Fountain,'[1] but in his Annunciations there is only the white lily. Memling, however, places an iris half hidden below the lilies in one Annunciation,[2] while in a ' Madonna with the Child '[3] there is also a single iris, though in this case the iris rises above the lilies.

The Master of Flémalle in his fine ' Saint Barbara '[4] places an iris in a vase beside the saint, where the white lily of a virgin martyr might have been expected.

The symbolism of the iris and the lily at first sight appears to be identical, and the substitution of the iris for the *lilium* seems to be the result of some confusion between ' lys ' and ' fleur-de-lys,' accentuated by the likeness between the iris and the lilies of the French royal standard with which the people of the Netherlands were familiar, since they were emblazoned on the shield of the Dukes of Burgundy.

In the mosaics of Ravenna, where the lily is used to indicate the delights of Heaven, it is

---

[1] Royal Museum, Antwerp. [2] Coll. Radziwill, Berlin.
[3] Royal Gallery, Berlin. [4] Prado, Madrid.

drawn in silhouette, showing three petals, and very closely resembles the ' fleur-de-lys ' of heraldry. The same convention born of the extreme difficulty of giving modelled form in utter whiteness, particularly in a medium un-fitted to express fine gradations of shade, is found in woven work, tooled leather, and em-broidery, and the common likeness of the imper-fectly-rendered *lilium candidum* and the iris to the sacred lily of the French and English royal standards, is sufficient to account for any in-decision as to which was precisely the Virgin's lily.   It is conceivable, too, that the artists of the Netherlands, when they painted a Madonna for their churches, set her in the midst of the iris which grew so thickly round their doors rather than limit her patronage to the white lily, which was still exotic and confined to some few convent gardens.   For the iris made their Lady more entirely their own—and so she would appeal more strongly to the emotions of the simple.

But in the Netherlands, in the fifteenth cen-tury, symbolism was usually very precise, and there does seem to be a slight difference in the use of the two lilies. The *lilium candidum* is used exclusively as the symbol of virginal purity, more particularly in relation to the fact that the Virgin Mary was a mother, but the iris, the royal lily, appears to be the emblem or attribute of the incarnate Godhead. Though Saint Bernard of Clairvaux had attributed the metaphor, ' I am . . . the lily of the valleys,' to the Virgin, Origen, the older and, in the North, weightier authority, held Christ to be the lily. In the ' Adoration of the Shepherds '[1] of Hugo van der Goes, where the symbolism all refers to the Child, there is no white lily, but the orange lily and the purple and white iris. In the Annunciation of Memling, the single iris below the lilies may be the emblem of the Prince of David's house who was to be born of virginal innocence—and it may have the same meaning where it rises above the lilies in the picture where the royal Child sits upon His mother's knee. It may also indicate royal birth in the ' Saint Barbara ' of the Prado. She was the daughter of a King, but in this painting has no crown or other attribute of royalty. It is noticeable, too, that had there been a white lily in the vase it would have been difficult to dis-

[1] Uffizi, Florence.

E

tinguish this Saint Barbara from a figure of the
Virgin.

The idea of royalty in connection with the
iris received support from the constant recur-
rence of the 'fleur-de-lys,' accepted as an iris
(though some contend that the form, as a symbol
of royalty, came originally from Egypt and was
founded on the lotus), on royal crowns and
sceptres. Memling and his school used such
crowns as the symbol of divine majesty, placing
them upon the heads of God the Father,[1] of
God the Son,[2] and also on the head of the
Virgin Mary.[3]

Dante also appears to use the 'fleur-de-lys'
or 'fiordaliso' as a symbol of honour:

> '. . . Beneath the sky
> So beautiful, came four-and-twenty elders (signori)
> By two and two, with flower-de-luces crown'd.'[4]

Some commentators, taking the four-and-
twenty personages as the four-and-twenty canonical books of the Old Testament, consider

---

[1] 'Coronation of the Virgin,' shrine of Saint Ursula, Bruges.
[2] 'Christ surrounded by Angels,' Royal Museum, Antwerp.
[3] 'Madonna with the Child,' Marienpfarrkirche, Danzig.
[4] *Purga*, xxix. 81.

the crowns of flowers to be symbolical of the purity of the doctrine found within the books, holding a ' fiordaliso ' to equal the white lily as a symbol, but it is possible that the poet meant the formal fleur-de-lys upon a golden crown or the fresh iris blooms which would also form a crown of honour.

The iris is sometimes used symbolically in Italy, and there is in the Church of S. Spirito in Florence an ' Annunciation ' now usually ascribed to Pesello. Between Mary and the angel stands a vase from which spring three purple iris. This vase, on either side of which the figures bend, is not merely a variation of the vase of white lilies indicating the virginity of Mary which is seen in so many early Annunciations, but it is the same symbol developed and enriched, till it represents the dogma of the immaculate birth of Christ. The vase, in many cases transparent, typifies Mary, and the upspringing flower is the emblem of the incarnate Godhead.[1]

Ghirlandaio places the iris, violet and daisy, each growing up strongly and freshly from the

[1] *See* Chapter XIV., ' The Lily of the Annunciation.'

bare ground of the stableyard, in his 'Adoration of the Shepherds,'[1] and in a picture of the sixteenth century by Palmezzano of Forlì,[2] the Child, seated on His Mother's knee, holds a stem of iris as a sceptre; but, on the whole, the iris was little painted in Italy.

In art which is purely German the iris is very rarely used, though Albert Dürer painted a 'Madonna of the Sword-lily,'[3] but in Spain it holds an important place. Spanish art is poor in symbolism, though it recognized early and prized highly the white lilies of the Annunciation. Except, perhaps, for the flame-tipped dart of divine love, there seems to be no symbol of truly Spanish origin, and those used by Spanish artists were mostly taken from the art of the Netherlands. Flemish art was profoundly admired in Spain, and the Spanish were well acquainted with it, for there was naturally much intercourse between the two countries in the days before the Netherlands established their independence. Also Jan van Eyck visited Portugal and Spain in the train of his patron,

[1] Accademia, Florence.   [2] The Brera, Milan.
[3] The Rudolphinum, Prague.

Philip the Good of Burgundy, and from the Hispano-Mauresque types in some of the later work of the Master of Flémalle there is reason to think that he, too, had been in the peninsula.

The symbol of the Flemish painters which particularly appealed to the Spanish was the iris, which grew small and wild upon their own hills, and with a freer, heavier growth in the palace gardens, whose admirable water-works had been planned and executed by the despised Moors. They adopted the iris as the royal lily of the Virgin, the attribute of the Queen of Heaven, as the *lilium candidum* was the attribute of the Maid of Nazareth. The iris, therefore, was deemed particularly suitable as a detail in that most favourite Spanish devotional representation of the Virgin, an ' Immaculate Conception.' The Virgin, represented as the woman ' clothed with the sun and the moon beneath her feet,' is usually attended by child angels who carry roses, lilies, palm and olive. The purple iris is generally added, and sometimes the white lily is omitted and the iris only given. The Spaniards, therefore, attached the same idea of royalty to the iris as did the Flemings, but transferred the attributes from the royal Son to the crowned Mother, for in Spain it is not found as the attribute or the emblem of the Infant Christ.

Later, the whole Catholic Church seems to have accepted both the iris and the lily, and the mosaic altar-frontals of St Peter's in Rome bear a design in which the rose, the lily and the iris are united.

V

THE ROSE

ROSES, among the Romans, were the symbol of victory, of triumphant love, of the pride and pomp of life, and were by long association as pagan as the lily is sacred. The Madonna lily (*lilium candidum*) was the flower of the Virgin and of the virgin saints; the rose was the flower of Venus.

> 'And on hire hed, full semmly for to see
> A rose gerlond fressh and wel smelling.' [1]

In the ' Triumph of Venus,' by Cosimo Tura,[2] the goddess, who is in truth a modest-looking lady, fully draped and firmly girdled, wears a crown of roses, red and white. Beneath her cockle-shell is another picture,[3] the sea is ' sucking in one by one the falling roses, each severe in outline, plucked off short at the stalk, but em-

[1] Chaucer, *The Knight's Tale.*
[2] Schifanoja Palace, Ferrara.
[3] Botticelli, Uffizi.

71

browned a little as Botticelli's roses always are.'[1]

But the Church grudged Venus the flower. Roses, said Wilfred Strabo, were the flower of martyrdom. '*Rosæ martyres, rubore sanguinis,*' wrote Saint Melitus, Bishop of Sardes, in the second century, and Saint Bernard of Clairvaux found the rose to be a fitting symbol of the Passion of our Lord. But though the rose was red to the colour of blood, and fenced around with cruellest thorns, it had been so long associated with the joys of life that the world refused to recognize it as the flower of death. Only as the sign of the triumphant entry of the departed soul to Heaven was the symbol acceptable. Roses sprang from the blood of those who fell for their faith at Roncevaux (as indeed they sprang from the spilt blood of Adonis), but they were also the sign of victory over the pagan, and when the Virgin Mary was laid within her tomb it was in rejoicing that ' straightway there surrounded her flowers of roses which are the blessed company of martyrs.'[2]

[1] Walter Pater, ' Sandro Botticelli.'   [2] *Legenda Aurea.*

But the Church, always wise in matters æsthetic, did not insist upon the tragic significance of the rose. It was allowed to be still the symbol of love, but of divine love, and it is as the symbol of the love of God that it now decorates our churches in carvings of wood or stone, in the silver work of church ornaments and on embroidered vestments and altar frontals.

The rose has never been especially associated with the person of Christ. Origen, who held that the text which we render, ' I am the rose of Sharon,' was a self-description of our Lord, read the verse, ' I am the flower of the field,' so giving the Church no clear image. When in art an emblem was required to represent our Lord, the ancient catacomb devices of the lamb and the vine were employed. Any reference to Him under the metaphor of a flower was rare and usually vague, as the charming ' gold flower ' of the Blickling Homilies. ' Then the Queen of all the maidens gave birth to the true Creator and Consoler of mankind, when the gold-flower came unto this world and received a human body from S. Mary, the spotless Virgin.'

Or again as a fruit rising from the mystical rose:

> ' Now spring up flouris fra the rute
> Revert you upward naturally
> In honour of the blissit frute
> That raiss up fro the rose Mary.' [1]

There are some mediæval Latin hymns for the Nativity in which Christ is referred to as the rose springing from the lily. The simile, however, was by no means applied to Him exclusively, for in a Visitation hymn of the same period He is alluded to as the lily hidden in the rose. But though the rose is not often the emblem of Jesus Christ, both in literature and art it is used as the symbol of His love.

Saint Mectilda, in the discourse on the three perfumes of divine love, tells us that ' the first of these perfumes is the rose-water distilled in the still of charity from the most beautiful of all roses, the heart of our Lord,' [2] and repeatedly in ecclesiastical art, roses falling or fallen from Heaven, signify divine love. The lovely angels in Signorelli's ' Paradise ' [3] carry roses in their looped draperies and scatter them

---

[1] William Dunbar.   [2] *The Book of Spiritual Grace.*
[3] Orvieto Cathedral.

down upon the redeemed souls beneath, and in Botticelli's ' Coronation of the Virgin ' [1] the air is also full of roses, symbols of the love of God. And symbols of divine love are also the falling roses in that vision of Saint Francis which was so often painted by Spanish artists and called by them ' La Portincula.' [2] The saint, kneeling in his cell one winter's night, was much troubled by the memory of a fair woman. To overcome the temptation he went out and threw himself among the briars of the wilderness. He was rewarded by a vision of the Saviour, seated in glory, with the Virgin by His side, and as a token that his penitences were accepted the thorns bloomed with roses. In most renderings of the legend the mystical roses fall in a shower around him, and in Murillo's fine picture [3] the *putti* are energetically pelting the saint with blossoms. It was a subject painted *con amore* by the Spaniards, for—Assumptions apart—

[1] Accademia, Florence.

[2] The *Portincula* or *Porzuincola* (the little portion) built by Saint Benedict and rebuilt by Saint Francis was the first church of the Franciscan order. It is now enclosed by the Church of S. Maria degli Angeli, and, close by, the rose-bushes of the legend, still thornless, are shown.

[3] Prado, Madrid.

the traditions of art in Spain were distinctly gloomy and they seized where they could an excuse for colour. Even Zurburan succumbed to the roses.[1]

The roses which strew the floor of Heaven in a famous diptych [2] by an unknown English painter are also symbols of divine love. The panels show Richard II, who is presented to the Virgin by Saint John the Baptist, Saint Edmund and Saint Edward the Confessor. The roses round the Virgin's feet are pink and yellow, and heavier, handsomer flowers than those which are found in Italian pictures of the same period. For the rest, this Heaven is especially remarkable for the politeness of the blue-winged, blue-robed angels, who each, in compliment to their royal visitor, wear his badge—a white hart couchant, collared and chained or—upon the shoulder.

Red roses, said Saint Bernard, were symbolical of the Passion of our Lord, but neither in Church observances nor in art have they been generally adopted with that meaning. There is, however, a picture of the Christ-Child in Cadiz. He

[1] Cadiz.   [2] Wilton House.

holds the crown of thorns, and at His feet are the globe and the apple. All around, filling the background, are blood-red roses, symbol of the Passion which was to come.

This forecast of pain in the Spanish renderings of the Saviour's infancy is even more marked in a picture by Zurburan,[1] where in play He plaits a crown of rose thorns, the flowers lying beside Him and at His feet.

Divine love and divine passion, intermingled, may be what the roses indicate in many ' Adorations ' of great beauty where the scene is laid in a rose-garden In the ' Adoration ' of Neri di Bicci [2] the Holy Child lies surrounded by lilies and red and pale roses. The lilies signify His sinlessness and the roses apparently His love and passion. The little Saint John stands behind with a scroll on which is inscribed ' *ECCE AGNUS DEI.*'

There is a lovely picture [3] now ascribed to Botticini, where angels playfully sprinkle rose petals over the Infant Christ in a rose-trellised

[1] Museo Provincial, Seville.
[2] Florence. To be placed in the Riccardi Palace.
[3] Palazzo Pitti.

garden. 'They worship here always alone,
though there is no gate to the garden; the angels
have relinquished high Heaven for these delights; for the scent of these roses which they
pluck, and the Child has relinquished Heaven
for these roses, and the thorns which he shall
gather from them . . . the season of their
thorns is never over, and whilst it is the time of
roses in this picture, there is the forecast of
their thorns in it.' [1]

In the *Speculum Humanæ Salvationis*, a MS.
of the fourteenth century,[2] the Holy Dove is
depicted upon a rose. From the bosom of a
seated figure, which represents David or Jesse,
a rose tree issues. At the summit of the tree
there is a five-petalled rose, in the centre of
which, as in a nest, sits a dove, which represents
the Holy Ghost.

The design is founded upon the text of
Isaiah which has been paraphrased by Pope:

' From Jesse's root behold a branch arise,
  Whose sacred flower with fragrance fills the skies;
  Th' ætherial Spirit o'er its leaves shall move
  And on its top descends the sacred Dove.'

---

[1] Robert de la Condamine, *The Upper Garden*.
[2] In the Bibliothèque de l'Arsénal, Paris.

The rose represents Christ, the perfect flower of the human race, sprung from the root of Jesse, and the dove descends upon it as the Holy Ghost descended upon our Lord at His baptism in Jordan.

Saint Bernard, differing from Origen, identified the Virgin Mary with the flower of the field and also with the abstraction described as ' Wisdom ' in Ecclesiasticus, ' exalted like a palm tree in Engeddi and as a rose plant in Jericho.'

> ' Rosa Mystica, ora pro nobis ! '

prays the Church.

> ' Here is the Rose
> Wherein the Word Divine was made Incarnate,'

wrote Dante.

An English hymn composed about the year 1300 has the lines:

> ' Lavedy (Lady), flower of alle thing
> Rosa sine spina
> Thu bere Jhesu, hevene king
> Gratia devina.'

And nearly two centuries later William Dunbar wrote:

> ' Hevins distil your balmy showris:
> For now is risen the bricht day-stir
> Fro the rose Mary, flour of flowris.'

Therefore, in the decoration of churches dedicated to the Madonna, the rose frequently occurs. It does not supersede the lily, which was the flower especially consecrated to her, but it is found beside it. The Church of S. Maria Maggiore in Rome is ornamented along the aisles, above the side chapels, with a series of panels, gold on white, which show the floral emblems of the Virgin. The rose, the lily, the olive, the laurel and the vine alternate down the whole length of the church. The beautiful little chapel behind the shrine of the Santissima Annunziata, in the Church of the Annunziata in Florence, was decorated in the seventeenth century with inlaid and raised *pietra-dura* work. Each of the five onyx panels which form the walls has upon it an emblem of the Virgin—the sun, the moon, the *Stella maris*, the lily, and, most lovely of them all, the branch of roses below the words ' Rosa Mystica.' This rose is red, and, strangely enough, the red rose, rather than the white, was chosen to represent the Virgin. Wrote Guido Orlandi in 1292:

> ' If thou hadst said, my friend, of Mary,
> Loving and full of grace;
> Thou art a red rose planted in the garden;
> Thou wouldst have written fittingly.'

In the *Sarum Book of Hours*, by Philippe Pigouchet,[1] published in 1501, the huge rose held by the Virgin definitely illustrates her title of ' Rosa Mystica,' but those pictures of the early Florentine school, in which she holds a small red or white rose, show her as the ' *Madonna del Fiore*,' for as ' Our Lady of the Flower ' she had been installed patroness of the city of Florence. It would have seemed natural, since the lily was upon the shield of Florence, to have placed a lily, her own flower, in the Madonna's hand. But the city of Florence had passed through troubled times just before the revival of her art, and the silver lily on her shield had been replaced by one of crimson.

' Had through dissension been with vermeil dyed.' [2]

Rather than paint her with the crimson lily, Florentine artists gave her the rose, and she holds a white leafless rose in the dainty little picture by Fra Angelico which is now in the Vatican.[3]

[1] British Museum. [2] Dante.
[3] In France at the same period it was very usual to place a ' fleur-de-lys ' in the Madonna's hand. For instance, the beautiful statuette in silver gilt of the early fourteenth century, now in the Louvre, carries a ' fleur-de-lys ' of crystal in the right hand.

F

There was an odd fancy about the beginning
of the eighteenth century to represent the Virgin
Mary as *La Divina Pastora* feeding her sheep
with roses. The original picture with this
title was by Alfonso da Tobar.[1] He found
imitators both in Spain and France, and in
Southern Spain the popularity of the subject
still persists. There is a plastic group, nearly
life-size, in the Church of S. Catalina in Cadiz.
The Virgin is dressed *à la Watteau* with a
beribboned crook and a rose-wreathed hat.
She feeds with roses and lilies the sheep and
lambs gambolling round her knees; an almond
tree flowers above, and the Christ-Child, dressed
as a small shepherd boy, stands in front. It is
all pink and white, gay and dainty, in a corner
of the austere whitewashed convent chapel
which has Murillo's beautiful ' Marriage of
Saint Catharine ' above the altar. A similar
group, but more dignified in type and less frivo-
lous in detail, is in the Church of the Holy Trinity
at Cordova. They are strange artificial flowers
of that gloomy growth, Spanish Art.

[1] The Prado, Madrid.

VI

THE CARNATION

In early German devotional poems the *nelken*, the pink, carnation or gillyflower, is occasionally used as the simile of the Virgin. Conrad von Würtzburg writes:

'Thou art a fragrant gillyflower sprig.'

But it has been given no definite and individual status as a symbol.

Very frequently, however, in ecclesiastical art, more particularly that of Venice and Northern Italy, it is found where the rose might be expected. It is placed with the lily in a vase beside the Virgin, with the violet before the Infant Christ, and with the wild strawberries among the grass of Paradise.

In Germany the carnation is seen falling from above with heavenly roses, and occasionally, even, in spite of the written legend, it replaces the roses in Saint Dorothea's wreath.

It would appear, therefore, that the symbolism of the carnation is identical with that of the rose, and when, for any reason, the artist did not care to paint the rose, he substituted the carnation.

Each year thousands of carnation blossoms are brought to the Lateran Church in Rome on the feast-day of Saint John, and the people bring carnations, not roses, because by midsummer's day the blooming time of Roman roses is almost past. A scarcity of roses would seem one reason at least in the Venetian pictures of the fifteenth century why the carnation replaces the rose. Earth, even sufficient to grow a rose bush, was scarce in the seawashed city, but carnations then, as now, must have grown in pots on every balcony. So the Venetians painted their own familiar flower rather than draw the rose, as Carpaccio did his camels, from descriptions furnished by observant travellers.

In the Netherlands and Germany artists probably preferred the carnation to the rose. It is more precise in shape, neater in its habit of growth, richer in colour than the rose, and therefore more in the spirit of Northern art, which liked to express definite and closely-reasoned symbolism with distinct bright colours and sharply-realized form. In the South, the artists, more concerned with the depicting of the soul than with the outer shell of things, more poetical and also more vague and less accurate in their symbolism, were better pleased with the more elusive charms of the loosely-petalled rose.

In an 'Adoration' by Botticelli [1] the Holy Child lies among violets, daisies and wild straw-berries, and the background is filled with freely-growing roses, drawn apparently from memory, not life. The roses signify the divine love which impelled the Saviour of the world to be born as a human Child. In the same subject by Hugo van der Goes [2] three carefully-painted carnations are placed in a crystal vase, and are symbols of the divine love of the Holy Trinity by which God the Son became incarnate, the crystal vase in Northern art typifying the Im-maculate Conception.

But in the Sienese and Florentine schools

[1] Private apartments, Pitti Palace, Florence.
[2] Uffizi, Florence.

also the carnation is sometimes found, and very rarely in the same picture as the rose.[1]   Therefore it would seem conclusive that when the painter of the Church did not care to use the rose because, probably, of its association with Venus and scenes profane, he was free, if he chose, to use the carnation as its substitute.

Strangely enough, the most famous carnations in the history of art, those two which have given the name of ' The Master with the Carnations ' to the anonymous Swiss painter of the fifteenth century, seem to have no symbolical significance.   The picture [2] shows Saint John the Baptist preaching to King Herod from the text: ' It is not lawful for thee to have thy brother's wife.'   The King is in his chair of state and the ladies of his court are seated upon cushions on the tesselated pavement before the pulpit.   Directly below the pulpit lie the two pinks; one is white and one red.   Possibly, since roses, according to Saint Melitus,[3] Wala-

[1] An exception is the Assumption by Fungai in the Belle Arti of Siena, where white roses and red carnations fill the tomb. The prejudice appears to have been against the red rose.
[2] Kunst Museum, Bern.
[3] ' The Key ' of Saint Melitus.

frid Strabo [1] and Saint Mectilda,[2] are the symbols of martyrdom, the carnation may foreshadow the approaching death of the preacher, but they are more probably simply a detail to give verisimilitude to the composition, as is the dog that worries a bone in the ' Dance of Salome ' by the same master.

[1] ' Hortulus,' Walafrid Strabo.
[2] ' Spiritual Grace,' Saint Mectilda.

VII

GARLANDS OF ROSES

'LET us crown ourselves with rose-buds,' [1] cried the revellers in the Book of Wisdom, and at Roman feasts host and guests alike wore roses on their hair or in garlands round their necks.

So in the heavenly mansions, where life is a perpetual feast, unfading roses crown the elect. Wreaths of roses are the symbol of heavenly joy and are worn alike by angels and by the human souls who have entered bliss.

An early Christian prisoner dreamt that he was already in Heaven:

'Towards us ran one of the twin children who, three days before, had been decapitated with their mother. A wreath of vermilion roses encircled his neck and in his right hand he held a green and fresh palm.' [2]

[1] The Wisdom of Solomon ii. 8.
[2] *Passio S.S. Jacobi, Mariani et aliorum martyrum in Numidia.*

Beneath Byzantine influence the rosy wreaths turned to crowns of jewels, and in the period between Constantine and Justinian crowns were considered strictly necessary for the guests at the heavenly feasts. But when the King of Heaven Himself was present all reverently uncrowned, and it is with their crowns in their hands that the twelve apostles stand, and the four-and-twenty elders in the mosaics of Rome and Ravenna. In the Neapolitan mosaics in the Chapel of Santa Restituta eight figures, apparently of martyrs, hold large crowns resembling a victor's wreath, and the graceful virgin saints on the wall of S. Apollinare Nuova each carries her wreath.

The tall, grand angels of the mosaics have neither wreaths nor garlands. They have gained no crown because no strife has ever troubled their serenity. They stand tall and straight, haloed, with spear-like wands in their hands.

After the twelfth century, however, the apostles and martyrs no longer carry the crown of victory, but it is the angels who wear wreaths, usually wreaths of roses, which are the symbol of heavenly joy. And, alas! what a lowering in type there was from the grand, dignified beings who guard the throne of Mary, on the wall of S. Apollinare Nuova, to the childish, peeping, rose-crowned little attendants which crowd behind her chair in pictures of the Sienese, Umbrian and early Florentine schools. The archangels still keep some dignity, but the sweet little doll-like creatures, rose-crowned and golden-winged, of Fra Angelico seem an inadequate representation of the hosts of Heaven.

But a magnificent strong-limbed angel of the Byzantine type would have overshadowed the slight, transparent-fleshed Madonna whose physique showed traces of the asceticism which went towards the making of a saint. So the angels, denied grand and vigorous frames, were decked with dainty robes and crowns of roses. Paul Bourget writes:

'Ce double et contradictoire Idéal, c lui d'une extase monastique conquise dans le martyre des sens et celui d'une beauté qui parle au sens, semble avoir co-existé dans le Pérugin

et dans les peintres qui l'ont précédé ou accom-
pagné, particulièrement dans Benedetto Bonfigli, dans Eusebio da San Giorgio, dans Gian-
nicola Manni et quelques autres dont la Pina-
cothèque de Pérouse enferme les œuvres. Ce
rêve complexe a son symbole dans les anges de
Bonfigli, couronnés de roses, comme les impies
dont parle l'Ecriture " Couronnons-nous de roses
avant qu'elles ne soient flétries," comme les con-
vives aussi des banquets paiens " Respirons
les roses tant qu'elles ressemblent à tes joues.
Embrassons tes joues tant qu'elles ressemblent
à tes roses." Mais ces pauvres anges aux
cheveux fleuris tiennent dans leurs mains les
instruments de la Passion du Sauveur, et une
pitié douloureuse noie de rouge leurs douces
prunelles où roulent de grosses larmes.' [1]

But blissful souls as well as angels wear
roses. In the Paradise of Simone Martini,[2]
Saint Peter with his key has opened the gate
of Heaven and two angels standing by crown
with roses each soul as it enters.

And more particularly those souls are crowned

[1] *Sensations d'Italie.*   [2] S. Maria Novella, Florence.

who in their earthly life could rejoice in their faith even when overwhelmed with troubles. Symbol of holy joy is the crown of roses which Saint Cecilia wears. Her legend, like other legends of the Early Church, is both more poetic and more allegorical than those which originated in later times.

Saint Cecilia lived in virginity with her husband Valerian, who, through love of her, became a Christian and was baptized.

'And returning home he found Cecilia in her chamber conversing with a glittering angel . . . and he held in his hand two crowns of roses and lilies, and he gave one of them to Cecilia and the other to Valerian.

'And on the morrow, when Tibertius came to salute his sister-in-law Cecilia, he perceived an excellent odour of lilies and roses, and asked her, wondering, whence she had untimely roses in the winter season.' (That is, whence came her holy joy during the season of persecution.) 'And Valerian answered that God had sent them crowns of roses and lilies but that he could not see them till his eyes were opened and his body purified' (by baptism).

Then follows the account of the conversion of Tibertius and the deaths of all three martyrs.

The ' Second Nonne ' told the legend of the saint very prettily to the Canterbury pilgrims:

> ' Thou with thy gerlond wrought of rose and lilie
> Thee, mene I, maid and martir Seint Cecilie.'

And her story appears to have been popular, though strangely enough she has never ranked in popularity with Saint Margaret, Saint Catharine of Alexandria, or Saint Barbara, notwithstanding that her story is certainly better authenticated than theirs, the historical details of her martyrdom having been proved beyond dispute. But she is essentially a Roman saint, her body lying in Trastevere on practically the spot where she suffered martyrdom under Marcus Aurelius, and with the strange jealousy of Italian cities she was almost ignored by Siena, Florence and Venice till Raphael, Roman in all his sympathies, painted the fine picture now in Bologna. In this picture, where she appears as the patroness of Music, she has no roses, but Luini [1] dresses her head charmingly with white roses and anemones.

[1] The Brera, Milan.

More fortunate than Saint Cecilia, Saint
Dorothea is beloved in almost all Christian
countries, for coming from Cappadocia there
could be neither vauntings nor heart-burnings
on her account in the Christian cities of Europe.
She too wears the roses of her legend.

' Send me then some roses from the Paradise
of your Christ,' scoffed the noble youth, Theophilus, as she passed to execution. At the
moment of death an angel appeared with three
roses and three apples. ' Take them to Theophilus,' said the saint, and Theophilus, believing,
died a martyr.[1]

Saint Dorothea is usually painted with both
apples and roses, symbols of the good works
of a Christian life and of the holy joy even in
the hour of death, which, reported to Theophilus,
astonished and finally converted him. She is
very popular both in the Low Countries and in
Germany. There is a charming triptych at
Palermo, the best picture Sicily possesses, attributed usually to Mabuse. On one wing
Saint Dorothea is depicted seated on the ground
with her lap full of red and white roses, a quaint,

[1] *Legenda Aurea.*

compact little figure, not a slender Italian maiden, supported by angelic visions, already half in Heaven, but of the sturdy Flemish type, who, having with clear brain calculated the cost, sets herself with stoicism to endure the pain which would be rewarded by the martyr's crown of unfading roses.

Curiously enough, the Virgin's crown is usually of gold and precious stones, though in one of Velasquez's rare religious pictures, ' The Coronation of the Virgin,' [1] God the Father places upon her head a wreath of red and white rose blooms. In the best period of Italian art the Virgin wears no crown except at a ' Coronation,' when most often it is of gold. In Germany the crowns are large and heavily jewelled, and in the Netherlands a jewelled fillet was very generally placed upon her hair. A notable and beautiful exception to these fillet-like coronets is the magnificent symbolical crown of jewels and fresh flowers which she wears as Queen of Heaven in Hubert van Eyck's ' Adoration of the Lamb.' [2] It was only in late art, that is, after the sixteenth century, that representations

[1] Prado, Madrid.   [2] Ghent Cathedral.

of Mary with the Child in her arms, as Queen of
Heaven, or as ' La Purissima,' became common.
Previously she had been painted as a human
mother with the sorrows of her motherhood
still upon her. As the mother, the greatest
of whose seven sorrows has not yet come, she
would not yet carry the rose crown which symbolized joy, even though it were heavenly joy,
and by the time religious sentiment demanded
representations of Christ's mother, risen to glory,
all sorrow past, the Church had decided to depict her as the woman ' clothed with the sun
and upon her head a crown of twelve stars.'

Akin to the wreaths of roses worn by angels
and saints are the hedges and rose-trellises of
Paradise.

Dante pictures Heaven as one great and
marvellous rose-bloom:

> ' How wide the leaves
>   Extended to the utmost, of this rose; [1]
>   . . . . . . which in bright expansiveness
>   Lays forth its gradual blooming, redolent
>   Of praises to the never wintering sun.' [2]

But the artists of the Church have usually de-

[1] *Paradiso*, xxx. 114.   [2] *Ibid.* 121.

picted Heaven not as a rose but as a rose-garden; and as a second and more perfect Eden rather than as the Holy City, the stupendous piece of jeweller's work described in the Revelation of Saint John. A few Flemish and German artists have attempted to realize the jasper wall, the 'pure gold like unto clear glass,' and the 'foundations garnished with all manner of precious stones,' but for the majority of artists on both sides of the Alps Heaven was a paradise, a garden. The prophet Esdras describes it in detail:

'Twelve trees laden with divers fruits,

'And as many fountains flowing with milk and honey, and seven mighty mountains, whereupon there grow roses and lilies.' [1]

The Byzantine *Guide to Painting* [2] directs that Paradise be depicted as 'surrounded by a wall of crystal and pure gold, adorned with trees filled with bright birds,' so combining both visions of the home of the blessed.

But Western art usually paints Heaven simply as a garden with twelve or six fruit trees,

[1] 2 Esdras ii. 18-19.
[2] Written by the monk Dionysius of Mount Athos in the twelfth century. Translated by M. Didron.

G

little fertile mounts, and grass thick with flowers, among which lilies and roses predominate.

The celestial meadow of Hubert van Eyck [1] has grouped trees as in a park and bushes covered with roses, and there are roses on bushes and trellises, crowns of roses and roses woven into swinging garlands in that most alluring of all painted paradises set by Benozzo Gozzoli upon the walls of the Palazzo Riccardi.[2] ' Roses and pomegranates, their leaves drawn to the last rib and vein, twine themselves in fair and perfect order about delicate trellises; broad stone-pines and tall cypresses overshadow them; bright birds hover here and there in the serene sky; and groups of angels glide and float through the glades of an entangled forest.' [3]

It is a paradise after the own heart of a Medici, in which no monotony, no boredom need be apprehended, full of gay and witty folk and the most gorgeous angels that were ever seen.

The roses of Paradise must not be confused with the rose hedge or trellis so often placed behind the Virgin by the early German schools.

---

[1] Adoration of the Lamb, Ghent Cathedral.
[2] Florence.   [3] Ruskin, *Modern Painters.*

These hedges indicate the ' Hortus Conclusus '
and identify the Virgin with the bride of the
Canticles by recalling the verse, ' A garden enclosed is my sister, my spouse.' This enclosure
is sometimes fenced merely by a row of flowers,
sometimes by a fortress-wall, and is often an
elaborate garden. An early instance by a master
of the Middle Rhine,[1] dating from about 1420,
gives eighteen recognizable species of flowers
and ten varieties of birds. The Madonna sits
reading beneath a tree. One saint gathers
cherries and another draws water from a fountain. Saint George, Saint Michael and a young
man chat beneath a tree, and a pretty young
saint with flowers in her hair teaches the little
Christ to play the psaltery. Other gardens
contain no flowers but the various objects used
as similes of the Virgin—the Tower of Ivory,
the Closed Door, the Sealed Fountain, etc.
Very often there is merely a trellis with roses
climbing up it, and the flowers which express the
virtues of Mary, the lily, violet and strawberry,
grow at her feet. The thorns on the roses are
carefully drawn, even accentuated, illustrating

[1] Town Museum, Frankfort-on-the-Maine.

the verse, ' As a lily among thorns, so is my
love among the daughters;'[1] but in spite of
the thorns the general significance of these
roses also is joy and delight.

In the Netherlands, where theologians occupied themselves less with this second chapter
of the Song of Solomon, Madonnas set *en plein
air* are scarcely found. The van Eycks and
Memling inaugurated the fashion of arranging
their devotional groups in chapel-like niches,
or in the aisle of some large church. Any garden
there is is seen in 'glimpses between pillars
or through windows, and has no mystical
meaning.

In the work of Botticelli and his school we
again see enclosed gardens of roses, but these
are rather gardens of adoration, for in the centre
the Virgin kneels before the divine Infant. As
in all Adorations the symbolism refers to the
Child, and these roses symbolize the Divine
Love which sent Him to this earth, and are not
the attributes of Mary or an indication of the
joy in Heaven. A true *hortus conclusus* of
Italian origin is that of Stefano da Zevio or da

[1] The Song of Solomon ii. 2.

Stefano da Zevio   *Photo Anderson*

THE 'ENCLOSED GARDEN' OF THE VIRGIN
(Royal Museum, Verona)

[*To face page* 100

Verona.[1] The Virgin, with the Child upon her knee, sits upon the ground in a carefully walled in garden, of which the only other human occupant is Saint Catharine, who strings a crown of roses. The garden is full of birds and bird-like angels, and in one corner is the ' sealed fountain ' of the Canticles.

As a general rule, roses massed together, in garlands, in baskets, or thickly growing, are the symbols of heavenly joys, and single roses are the symbols of divine love. But there is one single rose which is also the symbol of joy—it is the golden rose which is the gift of the Popes. Durandus writes: ' So also on the Sunday, Lœtare Jerusalem, the Roman Pontiff beareth a mitre, beautified with the orfrey, on account of the joy which the golden rose signifieth, but on account of the time being one of sadness, he weareth black vestments.[2]

' St Leon is seen upon the *châsse* of Charlemagne [3] with the golden rose in his right hand. The golden rose being the image of Heaven, according to the Liturgy, it became, in the hands

---

[1] Museum, Verona.   [2] *Rat. Off.*, iii. 18.
[3] *Trésor* of Aix la Chapelle.

of the Pope, the equivalent of a benediction.
One remarks that, in the epoch of which we
speak, the very poetical rite of the golden rose,
most ancient in the Church, had just acquired
a new celebrity. The sending of the symbolical
flower had replaced, in the Roman court, that of
the keys of confession, and Innocent III had just
consecrated a discourse to explain its mysterious
signification.' [1]

The sending of the golden rose was a very
old custom, dating at least from the time of
Gregory the Great. The rose was solemnly
blessed by the Pope on the fourth Sunday in
Lent and sent by him to some sovereign, church
or community. Urban V first made the ceremony annual about 1366.

This rose, symbol of the Church's blessing,
was often a thing of beauty and fine workmanship. Stefano del Cambio describes that one
which was sent in his time to Florence.

' On Easter Sunday morning, the 2nd of
April 1419, Pope Martin V, after having per-
formed Mass, gave the golden rose to our magnificent Signoria, in remembrance of the honours

[1] Arthur Martin, *Mélanges d'Archéologie.*

paid him by the Florentine people. . . . Our Signoria then returned to their palace with all the court of Cardinals and Prelates and the aforesaid rose bush, which was a golden branch with leaves of fine gold. On it were nine roses, and a little bud on top of the nine, which contained spices, myrrh and balsam.' [1]

Sometimes the ' rose ' was a whole rose bush about two feet high and covered with leaves and flowers. Two such bushes, one thornless, the gift of Pope Alexander VII, and the other, with long sharp thorns, though curved harmlessly downward, presented by Pius II, are still treasured by grateful Siena.

[1] Opera del Duomo.

VIII

THE COLUMBINE

WE read in Isaiah: 'And there shall come forth a rod out of the stem of Jesse, and a Branch shall grow out of his roots; and the Spirit of the Lord shall rest upon him, the Spirit of wisdom and understanding, the Spirit of counsel and might, the Spirit of knowledge and the fear of the Lord.' [1]

'These words were addressed to the Messiah. The Divine Child was therefore clothed with the Spirit of God, whose faculties are seven in number, for He possesses as His peculiar gifts, wisdom, understanding, counsel, strength, knowledge, piety and fear.

'This subject has frequently been portrayed by Christian artists. A tree springs from the bowels, the breast or the mouth of Jesse. The

[1] Isaiah xi. 1-2.

symbolic trunk spreads to the left and right, throwing forth branches bearing the Kings of Judah, the ancestors of Christ; at the top, seated on a throne, or the chalice of a gigantic flower, is the Son of God. Surrounding the Saviour, and forming as it were an oval aureole, seven doves are ranged one above the other, three on the left, three on the right, and one at the top. . . . These doves, which are of snowy whiteness, like the Holy Ghost, and adorned like him with a cruciform nimbus, are simply living manifestations of the seven gifts of the Spirit. The Holy Ghost is drawn under the form of a dove; each of the seven energies distinguishing Him is also figured under the same type.'[1]

These little doves surrounding the figure of Christ, as a man or as an infant, occur very frequently in the French miniatures of the thirteenth and fourteenth centuries, and are found upon the windows in the cathedrals of S. Denis, Chartres, Amiens and Beauvais, and in many other French churches.

It was an essentially French development

[1] *Christian Iconography*, Didron.

of Christian symbolism, and it is in Flemish
art, which drew its inspiration from the French
Renaissance, that we first find, not the little
white doves, but the columbine flower. The
columbine grows wild in most countries of
Europe and is usually dark blue in colour.
Each of its five petals is so shaped that it
is really very like a little long-necked dove.
The little doves are only five in number,
but the Flemish painters take each flower, not
each petal, as the symbol, and give seven
blooms upon each plant. There are six, and
the edge of the seventh is just showing, in the
mystical crown worn by Hubert van Eyck's
' Queen of Heaven.' [1]

Strictly speaking, however, Mary has no
right to these symbols of the gifts of the
Spirit, for it was to the expected Messiah
that the divine gifts were promised. The
columbine is more correctly used by Hugo
van der Goes, who in his ' Adoration of
the Shepherds ' [2] places a columbine, with seven
flowers upon it, in a vase before the Infant
Saviour.

[1] Ghent Cathedral.   [2] Uffizi Gallery.

The seven gifts of the Spirit are according to Isaiah:

SAPIENTIA
INTELLECTUS
CONSILIUM
FORTITUDO
SCIENTIA
PIETAS
TIMOR.

And according to the Apocalypse:

VIRTUS
DIVINITAS (in the Vulgate)
SAPIENTIA
FORTITUDO
HONOR
GLORIA
BENEDICIO.

But, at the Renaissance, Faith, Hope and Charity were taken as the theological virtues, and to them were added the four moral virtues exalted in pagan times above all others, namely, Prudence, Justice, Temperance and Strength.[1]

In a picture by Jörg Breu of the Virgin with the Child and two saints,[2] a vase of columbine, the only flowers introduced, is placed

[1] *Christian Iconography*, Didron.
[2] Kaiser-Friedrich Museum, Berlin.

in the foreground just below the Child, who stands on His Mother's knee.

Beside the vase is a sort of casket, out of which seven little cupid angels take seven scrolls. On the respective scrolls are inscribed: FIDES, SPES, CHARITAS, JUSTICIA, PRUDENCIA, FORTES. The seventh is blank, reserved, perhaps, for TEMPERANCE. A crowned saint, seated beside the Virgin, holds upon her knee a scroll on which is written ' AVE REGINA,' and above the Virgin's head hover two *putti* with a heavy crown. It is therefore to the Mother, rather than to the Child, that devotion is directed, and the seven Gifts are to be taken as her attribute.

In 1475 the ' Adoration of the Shepherds ' by Hugo van der Goes was brought to Florence by Tommaso Portinari, for the Chapel of the Hospital of Santa Maria Nuova. Its technique excited the greatest interest among the artists of Italy, and the vase of columbine in the foreground may have first drawn their attention to this symbol. Cosimo Rosselli, perhaps the last of the Florentine symbolists, painted it among the daisies, strawberries and jasmine-shaped

flower in the ' Madonna with the Child and SS.
Peter and James,' ' commissioned in 1492. After
the fifteenth century it is fairly frequent in
Italian art. Two of the most charming of the
Madonna pictures now in the Brera, ' The Virgin
and Child with the Lamb,' by Sodoma, and
' The Virgin of the Rose-hedge,' by Luini, both
introduce the columbine. But the Italian artists
use it vaguely, as the flower of the dove, the
flower in some degree sacred to the Holy Ghost,
and lost sight of the original connection with
the seven Gifts of the Spirit. Luini, who is
careless with his symbolism, though painting
flowers exquisitely, uses the columbine also as
an accessory in the famous portrait known
as ' La Colombina,' ' but here, of course, it is
simply a graceful flower in the hand of a fine
woman.

It is most unusual to find any flower used
symbolically in scenes representing the Passion
of our Lord. Should plants or shrubs be there,
it is merely as an indication that the place of
Crucifixion was beyond the walls, and that the
place of burial was a garden. They have no

' Uffizi Gallery. ² St Petersburg.

special meanings as symbols. An exception is
the ' Entombment ' [1] of Hans Schüchlin of Ulm.
From a rock in the foreground springs a plant
of columbine with three drooping flowers. On
a smaller plant at the side are four more blossoms,
making up the mystic seven. There are only
these columbines and a little short grass. On
the step of the tomb lies the crown of thorns
which has fallen from the head of the dead
Saviour as the disciples lower His body to the
grave.

The seven blooms of the columbine appear
again in the Thomas-altar [2] by the master of
the Bartholomew-altar, who painted during the
first twenty years of the sixteenth century. It
is a disagreeable picture, the types poor and the
action of the doubting Thomas, as he thrusts his
hand into the Saviour's wound, distinctly brutal.
But all round the feet of the risen Saviour lie
flowers scattered on the broad stone step.
There are again the seven heads of the columbine,
snapped off short and showing scarcely any
stalk; there are the violets of humility and the
daisy, often seen with the violet as the symbol

[1] Tiefenbronn Church.   [2] Wallraf-Richartz Museum, Cologne.

of perfect innocence in Adorations of the Infant Christ, but rare when He is represented as a grown man. There is also the strawberry flower but not the fruit.

After the sixteenth century the columbine seems to have dropped from Christian symbolism, and in modern religious art it has no place.

IX

THE OLIVE

' Strew thrice nine olive boughs
On either hand; and offer up thy prayer,' [1]

counselled the Greeks when conscious that the
deities were offended.

The olive was the gift of Pallas. The tale
ran that in the reign of Cecrops both Poseidon
and Athena contended for the possession of
Athens. The gods resolved that whichever of
them produced the gift most useful to mortals
should have possession of the land. Poseidon
struck the ground with his trident and straightway a horse appeared. But Athena planted the
olive and the gods thereupon decreed that the
olive was more useful to man than the horse,
and gave the city to the goddess, from whom it
was called Athenæ.[2]

But the symbolism of the olive, founded

[1] Sophocles, *Œdipus Coloneus.*
[2] Smith's *Classical Dictionary.*

112

upon its healing qualities and its oil's well-known property of calming roughened water, was not only Grecian: it was wide-spread, and the Romans used it politically as well as religiously. Their heralds carried olive on an embassy of peace, and the custom lingered in Italy through the Middle Ages; Dante describing how the multitude 'Flock round the herald sent with olive branch.'

In Christian art the olive also invariably represents peace or reconciliation, and it is first found in the Catacombs, where there is a curious painting of the mystic fish which swims towards the Cross with a sprig of olive in its mouth. The fish, by the well-known anagram, represents Christ, who, through the Cross, brings peace on earth.

A dove with an olive twig in its beak is also found upon early Christian tombs. And then, as Tertullian says, ' it is a symbol of peace even older than Christianity itself ' [1]—the herald of the peace of God from the very beginning. Sometimes the word itself, ' Pax,' [2] is added, thereby marking the sense beyond all possibility of dispute; viz., that it is meant to assert of the

[1] *De Baptismo*, c. viii.   [2] See title-page.

H

soul of the deceased that it has departed in the peace of God and of his Church.[1]

Tertullian refers, of course, to the dove sent forth by Noah which returned across the waters, and ' Lo! in her mouth was an olive leaf plucked off,' sign that the wrath of God was appeased. The dove, bearing the twig of olive, executed in coloured marbles, occurs repeatedly in the decoration of Saint Peter's. Here the dove represents the Church bearing the Gospel message of peace to the world. The same emblem is found in the decoration of St John Lateran, and Pope Innocent X. incorporated it with his coat of arms.

The olive naturally appears as an attribute in allegorical figures of Peace. One of the earliest and most famous of these figures is in Ambrogio Lorenzetti's great fresco entitled ' Good Government.' [2] The golden-haired Peace, who wears a white robe, is crowned with olive, and carries an olive branch in her hand. She has a beauty of her own, but compared with the more virile figures in the composition, Fortitude, Prudence, Temperance and Justice, she is a

[1] Northcote and Brownlow, *Roma Sotterana*.
[2] Palazzo Pubblico, Siena.

little heavy and inert, a little wanting in interest, as the citizens perhaps would have found their daily life were they condemned to days of peace.

In small, fierce Siena the olive was a very favourite symbol and found more frequently than any other. One of the most curious characteristics of religious art is the inexactitude with which it reflects a people's mood, for the ideal upon the wall above the altar is often just precisely that to which they do not strive. When the Medici were in power and Florentine social life was at its worldliest, simplicity and purity, almost austerity, were demanded of the artist, and the lily was the favourite symbol. Murillo painted Madonnas to the Church's order, sweet and forgiving, kind to indulgence, almost voluptuous, at a moment when not only the devotions of Jews and heretics but the private life of every citizen of Seville was under stern control. And in Seville, with inquisitorial fires blazing, the Virgin had as attribute the rose of love and charity. So the turbulent Sienese, who, when no enemy knocked at the gates, fought with one another, loved a still and peaceful art. It was conservative, for they cared for

no novelty, no variety of subject, pose or action.
And their favourite symbol was the olive branch
of peace. The angel Gabriel almost invariably
carries olive,[1] Saint John the Evangelist [2] and
Saint Ansano,[3] their own saint, both hold
branches of it, and it crowns the blonde curls
of many a little angel.

In representations of the first and third
persons of the Holy Trinity the olive branch is
very rare. Upon some ancient crucifixes, however, where a hand holding a wreath represents
the Eternal Father, the wreath, though usually
of laurel, in some instances is formed of olive.
In the Crucifix of the tenth century, known as
the Crucifix of Lothair,[4] the wreath is distinctly
of olive, but since it encircles the Holy Dove the
olive is perhaps equally the attribute of the
Holy Ghost. In the Crucifix upon the Manual
of Prayer of Charles the Bald,[5] the wreath is of
laurel and there is no dove.

Mabillon speaks of a group of the Trinity in
human form, sculptured by order of Abelard

[1] Taddeo di Bartolo, Sano di Pietro, Francesco di Giorgio
Martini, Belle Arti, Siena.   [2] No. 160, Belle Arti, Siena.
[3] Stefano di Giovanni, Belle Arti, Siena.
[4] Trésor of Aix la Chapelle. [5] Trésor of the King of Bavaria.

at the Paraclete. In it the Father wore a closed crown, the Son a crown of thorns, and the Holy Ghost a crown of olive. The group has long since disappeared, and there seems no other instance of the Holy Ghost in human form being represented with the olive. A dove bearing an olive twig could not be an emblem of the Holy Ghost unless the bird's head were encircled with a halo.

But Christian art uses the ancient symbol of peace repeatedly when illustrating Christ's life upon earth. First we find the angel Gabriel bringing to the Virgin a branch of olive as token that his message is of peace. Sometimes he is also crowned with olive. He comes crowned with peace, and the branch in his hand foreshadows the reconciliation between God and man which is to come by the Child whose advent he announces.

The olive branch took precedence of the lily as the symbol carried by the announcing angel. Originated probably by Simone Martini, one of its earliest instances is in his Annunciation now in the Uffizi. In the Florentine school the simple stick carried by the herald angel evolved, as we have seen, through the fleur-de-lys to the stem of lilies. In Siena it was the meaning of the wand, rather than the wand itself, which was developed. The wand simply marked that Gabriel was a herald; that it was a message of peace and goodwill which he brought was shown by the grey-green leaves of the olive. As a symbol it was by no means of Simone Martini's own finding, for it was a very usual political symbol of the day, but he seems to have been the first to have placed it in the angel Gabriel's hand, and the school of painting in Siena whole-heartedly and faithfully adopted his device. The general trend of Sienese symbolism was to direct devotion to the incarnate Godhead rather than to Mary of Nazareth, and it is of Him, as the bringer of peace on earth, that the branch of olive tells, as elsewhere the white lily proclaims the virginity of the coming motherhood.

Then again, on that night when the angels sang of peace on earth and good-will towards men—

> . . . 'the meek-eyed Peace,
> She crown'd with Olive green, came softly sliding
> Down through the turning sphear.' [1]

---

[1] Milton.

In one of the most naïve and fascinating of all Botticelli's pictures[1] the angels crowned with olive hold up branches of it against the golden sky. Other angels, half distraught with joy, run with waving olive-sprays to greet the astonished shepherds.

The same subject is much more soberly treated by Sano di Pietro.[2] One angel, flying through the twilight, brings a twig of olive to the shepherd who is sleeping on the hillside.

There are many symbolical fruits placed in the hand of the Infant Christ. Botticelli paints a pomegranate, Mabuse a quince, Memling an apple, Il Moretto a pear, and each represents the individual artist's conviction as to what really was the unnamed fruit of the Tree of the Knowledge of Good and Evil which grew in the midst of Eden. The placing of the olive, symbol of reconciliation, where it might be confused with the fatal fruit which made that reconciliation so imperative was carefully avoided, and we rarely find the olive branch in

[1] 'The Nativity,' National Gallery.
[2] 'The Nativity,' Belle Arti, Siena.

the hand of the Child when seated on His mother's knee. And there was still another reason. He had Himself said: 'I come not to bring peace upon earth, but the sword,' therefore the earlier and more literal artists refused Him the symbol of peace, even as divine peace. There are, however, instances of the Christ-Child with the olive branch, of which the most important is the 'Holy Family' by Mantegna.[1] The Christ, a beautiful and dignified childish figure of three or four years old, stands on a sort of pedestal with the little Saint John. He holds a branch of olive in His right hand, upright like a sceptre, and in the other is the crystal orb which symbolizes sovereignty. Saint Joseph stands behind and the Virgin lays a rosebud at her Son's feet.

The Bringer of Divine Peace was an aspect of the incarnate Son of God on which Mantegna laid emphasis. In the 'Holy Family,' now in Dresden, painted about the same period, the little Saint John holds a branch of olive (from which two tiny side-sprays grow naturally in the form of a cross) as an attribute of the Holy Child.

[1] Collection L. Mond, London.

The olive branches of the 'Entry into Jerusalem,' like the olives of Gethsemane, were only accidentally allegorical. The villagers of the Mount of Olives cut down branches (presumably olive branches) 'and strewed them in the way.' With palm branches they would salute any popular leader, and it is scarcely to be believed that they definitely selected the olive and palm with the full understanding of the symbolism which the Christian Church attaches to them.

'The olive branches signify his office as peace-bringer and the palms his victory over Satan.'[1]

There is in the Catacombs a figure of the Virgin Mary praying between two olive trees. Her name is inscribed above her head. She is standing with raised hands in the early attitude of prayer, and these olive trees apparently symbolize 'the peace of God which passeth all understanding.' But after the twelfth century the Church had identified the personality of the Virgin with the figure of Wisdom eulogized in Ecclesiasticus, and the olives which are some-

---

[1] Durandus, *Rat. Off.*, vi. 47-9.

times found beside her refer to the verse which compares her to

' A fair olive tree in a pleasant field.' [1]

Botticelli painted a beautiful ' Madonna of the Olives ' for the Church of S. Spirito. Vasari writes of it: ' In S. Spirito in Florence he has painted a picture for the Chapel of the Bardi which is carefully executed and well finished, where there are some olives and palms painted with great love.' [2]   In another picture by Botti. celli [3] angels hold above the Virgin's head a lightly-framed crown of gold which is decorated with fresh sprays of lily, palm and olive.

The most popular of modern Italian representations of the Virgin and Child is very justly that painted by Niccolò Barabino [4] and entitled ' *Quasi Oliva Speciosa in Campis.*' Large branches of olive, painted also ' with great love,' are placed about the feet of the sweet-faced Mother, who peeps through her heavy white veil, and they almost hide the fruit of temptation which lies on the ground beneath.

[1] Ecclesiasticus xxiv. 14.
[2] *Lives of the Painters.*
[3] Corsini Gallery, Florence.
[4] Monza.

Martin Schöngauer

GABRIEL CROWNED WITH OLIVE BRINGS THE MESSAGE
OF RECONCILATION

(Print Room, Alte Pinakothek, Munich)

To face page 123]

One of the *putti* which fly round the feet of the Madonna in a Spanish 'Immaculate Conception' usually carries a branch of olive, and that, too, bears the same meaning. As an olive tree in a pleasant field she brings peace and consolation to mankind. She is the 'Mater Consolatrix.'

Sodoma painted a stately figure of Saint Victor,[1] with sword and palm, and the] little rose-crowned child-angel who supports his shield holds above it a branch of olive, symbol of the peace which to a Christian warrior should be the end of victory.

The same idea dominates the 'Judith'[2] of Botticelli. The slayer of her country's enemy returns thoughtfully home, satisfied but not exultant. In her right hand is her sword, carried low; upright, in her left, a branch of olive. Though her deed was bloody, she had brought peace to the land.

Flemish art neglects the olive, and except in the drawings of Martin Schöngauer,[3] whose grave gentle Gabriels wear olive crowns, it is seldom seen in Germany. The reason is easy

[1] Palazzo Pubblico, Siena.   [2] Uffizi, Florence.   [3] Munich.

to guess. The olive tree not growing in the North, the painters would be at a loss to find a branch from which to draw, and the people, unacquainted with the leaf, would scarcely recognize its hidden message of peace. In France it is seen less rarely. On the sculptured portal of the Cathedral of Amiens there is a curious rendering of the parable of the Wise and the Foolish Virgins. A withered olive tree, without fruit or leaves, grows by the side of the foolish maidens, and a healthy olive tree, laden with fruit and ready with abundance of oil, is beside those maidens who were wise.

But on the whole the olive is an Italian, and more particularly a Sienese, symbol, though Botticelli also loved the silvery leaves. In his magnificent ' Pallas taming the Centaur,' [1] painted for Lorenzo de' Medici, to commemorate his diplomatic victory over the King of Naples and the League in 1480, olive encircles the head of the lovely goddess and is wreathed about her dress. The surface meaning of the picture is that, by the arts of peace taught them by the beneficent goddess, men were enabled to over-

[1] Private apartments, Pitti Palace.

come the savagery of nature, typified by the centaur. But it also shows, allegorically, how the wise statesmanship of Lorenzo (with whose badge, rings interlaced, the gown of Pallas is ' semé ') guided the war-loving League, here figured as the centaur, into the ways of Peace.

X

THORNS

THORNS and thorn branches signify in general grief and tribulation, the word tribulation itself being derived from a Latin root signifying thistles or briars. But, according to Saint Thomas Aquinas, thorn bushes signify the minor sins, and growing briars or brambles those greater ones, ' quæ pungunt conscientiam propriam,' etc.

He is supported in his opinion by Saint Anselm, and both saints explain in this sense the words of Saint Paul, who wrote to the Hebrews:

' That which beareth thorns and briars is rejected and is nigh unto cursing, whose end is to be burned.'

The crown of thorns with which jesting soldiers crowned the Christ was in itself an emblem, or at least a parody, of an emperor's festal rose-crown. According to *The History*

of the Crown of Thorns of the Holy One,[1] the
first crown with which Jesus Christ was crowned
was made of white-thorn and was removed
before the Crucifixion and replaced by a second
de juncis marinis.

But in the great majority of scenes from the
Passion the crown is merely formed of large thorns
without any attempt to realize any particular
natural growth. In Germany, where Entomb-
ments and Pietàs were more often painted
than in other countries, the crown is frequently
green, in allusion, it is suggested, to the words:
' If these things be done in the green wood, what
shall be done in the dry? '

In these pictures the crown of thorns, if not
still upon the Saviour's head, is usually placed
very prominently in the foreground, marking
to some extent the divinity of the dead Christ,
for, since life had fled, there could be no
halo.

In Northern art the crown of thorns remains
always unchanged, the symbol of Christ's sufferings, but in at least one Italian Pietà,[2] the dry
prickles round the dead Christ's brow have

---

[1] Nierenberg.   [2] Mantegna, Belle Arti, Verona.

bloomed with delicate white briar-roses—an exquisite figure of Love's triumph over Pain.

Sometimes, in pathetic forecast, the Child Christ has the crown of thorns hung on His tiny wrist [1] or plays with it as with a toy, and in a very charming picture,[2] with less poignant and more pleasing symbolism, a waiting child-angel stands by with a wreath of the blue sea-holly.

In Spain the Christian faith was stern. Faith and suffering were more closely allied than faith and joy. They had no ' jesters of the Lord,' and their saints glorified God by self-inflicted pain rather than by acts of mercy. So their Christ in childhood was not a smiling, unconscious *bambino*, but a sad-faced child who wounds Himself with the rose-twigs which He twists into a crown. The rose-thorn tears His flesh but the roses lie beside Him and round His feet, for His griefs and sufferings were the outcome of His divine love. Both Zurburan [3] and Alonzo Cano [4] painted fine pictures on this theme.

[1] Botticelli, Poldi Pezzoli Collection, Milan.
[2] Botticelli, Borghese Gallery, Rome.
[3] Museo Provincial, Seville.
[4] Collection of the Duchess of Fife.

Zurbarán   THE CROWN OF THORNS   Photo Anderson
(Museo Provinciale, Seville)

To face page 128

There is a ' Coronation of the Virgin ' by
Hans Burgkmair,[1] painted in 1507, where beneath a cross-surmounted imperial crown Christ
wears the Crown of Thorns. In several of the
French fifteenth-century miniatures of the
Trinity in Glory, God the Son still wears the
Crown of Thorns, but this combination of the
two crowns is rare. It was, however, in reverent
remembrance of the thorn-crowned King of
the Jews that the Crusader, Godfrey de Bouillon,
twisted a thorn-branch round his coronet when
he was crowned King of Jerusalem. His bronze
statue, wearing this double crown, stands with
those of the other Christian kings guarding the
tomb of Maximilian in Innsbruck Cathedral.

Among modern symbolists, Holman Hunt
has used thorns with finest effect. In his
' Light of the World ' the Saviour wears again
the double crown, the thorns which symbolize
His sufferings intertwisted with the golden
crown of His divinity. He stands with the
lantern, which is the light of His Gospel, before
the closed door of the human heart, a door all
overgrown and blocked by the weeds and briars

[1] Royal Gallery, Augsburg.

I

which are the symbols of sin and things evil.
There is the poisonous hemlock, the ivy which
kills the tree that it embraces, thorns denoting
the lesser sins, and the brambles which are the
emblems of the greater ones. According to
Raban Maur the bramble is also an emblem of
the riches which destroy the soul.

In several modern pictures of ' The Good
Shepherd ' Christ is depicted as rescuing a lamb
caught by its wool in the briars of the wilderness.
The lamb, of course, is the emblem of an erring
soul, and the briars represent those sins which
hold it back from answering the Shepherd's
call.

In connection with the saints, the Crown
of Thorns is not used symbolically, except when
placed upon the head of Saint Catharine of
Siena,[1] to indicate her austerities. According
to the legend, Christ in a vision offered her a
crown of roses or a crown of thorns and she chose
the thorns. When it is carried by Saint Louis
of France it is to recall the fact that it was he
who brought to France, as her most precious
relic, the Holy Crown itself.

[1] Sassoferrato, Church of S. Sabina, Rome.

The tonsure was originally instituted to keep fresh in the memory the Saviour's Crown of Thorns. And in the ' Paradise ' of Fra Angelico [1] the monks are crowned with roses. Thus the emblem reverted to the original symbol. The Crown of Thorns was the parody of the rose-crown, symbol of rejoicing; the tonsure the reverent imitation of the thorny wreath, and angels at the entrance of Paradise change the tonsure for a wreath of roses.

In early German art the Virgin is often found seated in a garden of which each flower has its significance. Behind and around her there is usually a sort of trellis or bower covered with roses. The roses have very pronounced thorns, and the thorns are accentuated to recall that Mary is the lily and the bride of the Canticles, the ' Lily among thorns.' In an Assumption of Seghers [2] one of the attendant *putti* flies towards her with a single lily enclosed in branches covered with long-spiked thorns.

On the other hand, when the rose is the direct emblem, not the attribute of the Madonna, it

[1] Accademia, Florence.   [2] Uffizi, Florence.

has no thorns, for then it illustrates her title, ' *rosa sine spina.*'

The Roman Breviary likens the Virgin to the burning thorn bush in which Jehovah revealed Himself to Moses and the simile was cited by Bishop Proclus in a Mary-sermon preached in the fifth century. Though enwrapped in the all-consuming flame of divine love, she yet remains unharmed. It is only in German art that this simile has been pictorially translated. German artists were familiar with the idea through Conrad von Würtzburg's apostrophe to the Virgin:

> ' In the thorn bush on the bare field
> Moses, the hero of God
> Saw in a glow of bright fire
> The birth of our Saviour foreshadowed.
> In the blast of the flame
> It remained unaltered
> As if neither leaf nor twig
> Perceived the death-giving blaze.
> In this we may recognize
> The full magnificence of thy maidenhood.' [1]

And we find this burning Thorn Bush with the Ivory Tower, the Sealed Fountain, the Fleece

[1] *Der Goldene Schmiede.*

of Gideon and other emblems of the Virgin, in the fifteenth-century renderings of the *Hortus Inclusus* and in the background of the essentially German allegory of the Incarnation, known as the ' Hunting of the Unicorn.' There are some fine embroideries and tapestries of the fourteenth and fifteenth centuries in the Bavarian National Museum,[1] in which the burning thorn bush, with the other symbols of the Virgin's purity, are worked with most careful detail.

The burning bush, not particularly a thorn bush, but the ' bush ' of our Authorized Version, is now the chosen emblem of the Church of Scotland.

There were neither thorns nor thistles in Eden. It was not till the day when Adam fell that God laid a curse upon the ground: ' Thorns also and thistles shall it bring forth to thee.' Therefore thorns and thistles are in general the symbols of sin and death. A little German woodcut expresses eternal death with gruesome completeness: a skull, with the apple of damnation between its bare jaws, has round its brow a wreath of twisted thorns.

[1] Munich.

XI

THE PALM

THE Romans took palms for their symbol of
Victory. There is a sarcophagus in the Vatican
on which is carved a Roman conqueror with
captive barbarians kneèling before him, and the
winged Victory who crowns him with laurel
holds a palm in her left hand.

Simon Maccabees, after he had taken the
Tower of Jerusalem, entered it 'with thanks-
giving, and branches of palm trees and with
harps.'[1] And the seers of Scripture saw palms
in heaven: 'A great multitude, which no man
could number, of all nations, and kindreds and
people, and tongues, stood before the throne
and before the Lamb clothed with white robes,
and palms in their hands.'[2] 'These be they
that have put off the mortal clothing and put
on the immortal, and have confessed the name

[1] 1 Maccabees xiii. 51. [2] Revelation vii.

of God; now are they crowned and receive palms.' [1]

Palms were therefore the meed of martyrdom, the symbol of the martyrs' victory over death.

> ' . . . The angel said
> God liketh thy request,
> And bothe with the palme of martirdome,
> Ye shallen come unto His blissful rest.' [2]

During the first three centuries of Christianity Christian art concerned itself almost exclusively with the events recounted in the Old and New Testaments and the Apocryphal Gospels. ' But during the fourth century artists began to represent the acts of the martyrs, at the bidding of Saint Basil, who called to his aid illustrious painters of athletic combats, to paint with resplendent colours the martyr Barlaam, the crowned athlete, whom he found himself unable adequately to describe. . . . A fresco came to light in 1887, under the Church of SS. Giovanni e Paolo on the Celian Hill, which shows three Christians being put to death beneath

[1] 2 Esdras ii. 45.
[2] Chaucer, *The Second Nonnes Tale.*

the rule of Julian the Apostate, kneeling with eyes bound and hands tied behind their backs. This may be considered as the first representation of a martyrdom. . . .'[1]

Sixtus III (432-440), as is shown by the inscription which is read above the principal door of Santa Maria Maggiore, had had the instruments of their martyrdom painted only beneath the feet of the martyrs.

> ' Ecce tui testes uteri sibi proemia portant
> Sub pedibusque jacet passio cuique sua.
> Ferrum, flamma, ferae, fluvius, sævumque venenum
> Tot tamen has mortes una corona manet.' [2]

Thus in the fourth century there were representations of martyrdoms, and in the fifth century single figures of the martyrs more or less idealized, but they apparently carried the crown of victory, ' the crown of their high calling,' not the palm. But though the crown was generally used, the palm of the primitive Christian Church was not forgotten, for, as Cassiodorus, writing at the beginning of the sixth century, points out, it was palms which, in the eyes of the people, indicated those strong athletes who were vic-

[1] A. Venturi, *Storia dell' Arte Italiana.*   [2] *Ibid.*

torious, and advocates their use as a religious symbol.

Palms at this period seem to have been used as an emblem of the public games themselves. On the consular diptyches, the double tablets of ivory which a consul had carved to commemorate his entry into office, it was customary to put palms beneath the figure of the consul, among the bags of money and other objects that were supposed to represent the benefits which would accrue to the populace beneath his rule.

It was probably this secular use of the palm which excluded it from the symbolism of the Church during the early centuries, for it is palm trees not palm branches which are found in the early mosaics, notably those of S. Apollinare Nuova in Ravenna, where palm trees alternate with the figures round the frieze, and palm trees, according to St Ambrose, were not the symbol of victory but the emblem of the righteous man, ' for its roots are upon the earth but its head is lifted towards the heavens.'

But by the thirteenth century the public games had dropped from Italian social life, and religious art reverted once more to the palm

branch of the catacombs as the symbol of
a martyr's triumph over death. Durandus,
writing about the year 1286, unites the different
renderings of the palm's significance. He says:
‘ Martyrs are painted with the instruments
of their torture and sometimes with palms,
which signify victory, according to that saying:

‘ “ The righteous shall flourish like a palm
tree; as a palm tree flourishes, so his memory
shall be preserved.” ’ [1]

After the Renaissance martyrs were very
generally depicted with palms, either in place
of, or in addition to, the instruments of their
martyrdom. They varied in size and shape,
from the tiny closed palm no longer than a
human hand, used by Cimabue,[2] to the magnificent pedestal of palm branches on which Carpaccio has set his ‘ Saint Ursula in Glory.’ [3]
Saint Christopher, the giant saint, in considera-
tion of his size, was always allowed a whole
palm tree as his staff, but a whole palm tree, or
the tiniest scrap of its foliage, carried exactly
the same meaning.

The palm is also given occasionally to several

[1] *Rat. Off.*   [2] S. Cecilia, Uffizi.   [3] Accademia, Venice.

saints who have not suffered a violent death, but have been conspicuous for their victory over pain and temptation; for instance, Saint Francis, Saint Catharine of Siena and Saint Clare.

Even in the Catacombs two palms are some-times placed crossways, not on the tombs of martyrs only, but on other Christian tombs, to signify the victory of the cross. For life as a declared Christian in the early days of the faith was sufficiently difficult and perilous, even if it did not end in death at the hands of the executioner. In the same way the pilgrim who had overcome difficulties and encountered possible death on a journey of piety to the holy sepulchre was permitted to take the name of palmer when he ' brings home his staff en-wreathed with palm.'[1]

Meanwhile palms never fell into disuse as a secular symbol. When they appear on the seals and coins of emperors and kings they indicate entirely worldly power and authority, and it is not in recognition of sainthood that the winged genius presents Henri IV with palm and wreath

[1] Dante.

of laurel in the fine allegorical picture of his ' Entry into Paris after the Battle of Ivry.' [1]

In a hymn of Saint Augustine, Jesus Christ is designated the ' Palma bellatorum,' but, perhaps by reason of its pagan origin, and also because it has never been exclusively a religious symbol, Christ as the conqueror of sin and death is seldom depicted with the palm of victory. In a few devotional Crucifixions palms are placed crossways above the Saviour's head, and very rarely it is seen in the hand of the newly-risen Christ. He almost invariably carries instead the banner of the Resurrection with a scarlet cross upon a white ground. In one of the rare representations [2] where He holds a palm He holds also the banner in His other hand, and it is striking how the adding of the lesser symbol to the greater, an error the early masters carefully avoided, detracts from the dignity of the figure.

In the four canonical gospels, palms as a symbol are only mentioned once, the occasion being the entry of Jesus Christ ' riding lowly

[1] Rubens, Uffizi.   [2] Piero della Francesca, Uffizi.

upon an ass ' into Jerusalem before the feast of the Passover.

' They . . . took branches of palm trees and went forth to meet Him, and cried Hosanna! '

It was a respect paid to a reigning sovereign and would support the accusation of the Jews that He sought to make Himself a king.

The entry into Jerusalem is not an incident in the life of Christ which is used for devotional contemplation, though it occurred usually in the series of scenes from the life of Christ which were frequent in pre-Renaissance art, executed in carved wood, ivory and marble; and in the hands of the villagers of the Mount of Olives the palms signified, of course, simply triumph, for they had not yet gained the full Christian meaning of victory through the Cross.

In representations of the entry of Christ into Jerusalem, the palms are merely a historical detail, but it is a true symbol, in defiance of the probable fact, when the Saviour Himself is represented carrying the palm, as in the *Biblia Pauperum* of 1440.[1] It is then purely a symbol of His triumph over sin and death.

[1] At Heidelberg.

In this same edition of the *Biblia Pauperum* the palm is also, strangely enough, placed in the hand of Christ in the Ecce Homo; the ' reed in His right hand ' set there in mockery, changed to the victor's palm.

Occasionally the palm is given to the angel Gabriel when he comes from Heaven to announce the Saviour's approaching birth. ' Ave ' is his salutation to the Virgin, and in Roman fashion, as in salutation to a queen, he kneels with a lifted palm.

Spinello Aretino paints Gabriel with the palm. In his Annunciation at Arezzo [1] the angel is first seen above, flying with the palm from before God's throne. Below he kneels, the palm in his hand, before the Virgin. Ambrogio Lorenzetti [2] and others follow the same tradition, but the palm was soon superseded in Siena by the olive and elsewhere by the lily, which was adopted by painters of all nations as the flower of the Annunciation.

The *Legenda Aurea* of Jacobus de Voragine gives an account of the death and burial of the Virgin. The legend is said to be an invention

[1] SS. Annunziata.   [2] Belle Arti, Siena.

of the Gnostics, and there is reason to believe of Lencius in the second century.[1]

Shortly before the Virgin's death the angel Gabriel again appeared to her, and ' he gave her a branch of palm from Paradise which he commanded should be borne before her bier.'

This branch of palm was clearly the symbol of victory over sin, since she had passed a full lifetime in perfect sinlessness and her surpassing sorrows had entitled her to the reward of martyrdom.

The Legend continues:

' And the palm shone which he had left behind with great clearness; it was green like a natural branch and its leaves shimmered like the morning star.' The palm, therefore, is distinguished from the palms of the martyrs by being encircled with stars. A Sienese artist paints seven,[2] the sacred number, corresponding with the Virgin's sorrows; other artists give twelve, foreshadowing that there should be upon her head ' a crown of twelve stars.'

Usually, in Italian pictures of the death or ' Dormition ' of the Virgin, an angel, or Saint John

---

[1] Lord Lindsay.　　[2] Opera del Duomo, Siena.

the Evangelist, appears at her bedside carrying the palm. Northern art was almost entirely uninfluenced by the details given by Jacobus de Voragine of the Virgin's death and burial, and though in Germany ' The Death of the Virgin ' is a very favourite subject, the palm is never introduced. Saint John frequently, however, holds a lighted taper, and some form of the starry palm tradition may have drifted northwards, for the master of the Sterzing Altar [1] paints a cluster of star-shaped flowers in the hand of Saint John, who bends over the inanimate form of the Virgin.

Her body was carried by divine command to the valley of Jehoshaphat, ' and John bare the palm branch in front of it.'

This scene, too, belongs to Italian art, and usually makes a beautiful processional group. Saint John, with the privilege of a son, walks before the bier. Duccio di Buoninsegna [2] paints him with the closed narrow palm of a martyr. In the charming little long-shaped picture by Fra Angelico [3] the palm has its fan-shaped

---

[1] Sterzing, Rathaus.   [2] Opera del Duomo, Siena.
[3] Uffizi, Florence.

leaves spread wide and it shines as if it were of gold.

In the 'Immaculate Conception' of the Spanish school one of the attendant *putti* usually carries a palm. This may be the palm of victory over sin and death, or, following another authority, it may be a symbol of the Immaculate Conception, since it bears fruit at the same moment at which it flowers.[1]

According to Dr Anselm Salzer, O.S.B., 'The palm, when referring to Mary, is a figure of her victory over the world and its temptations, of her everlasting virtue, of her sovereignty in heaven, of the protection that she offers to mankind, of her triumphant motherhood and of the beauty of her soul.'[2]

[1] W. Menzel, *Christliche Symbolik.*
[2] *Die Sinnbilder und Beiworte Mariens in der deutschen Literatur und lateinischen Hymnenpoesie des Mittelalters.*

K ·

XII

THE ACANTHUS

ONE plant, the acanthus, which was very much
used by pre-Renaissance artists, seems to have
dropped later from the flora of symbolism.

Paradise was embowered, according to Saint
Paulino da Nola, in *floriferi caeleste nemus
paradisi*, and curving branches of acanthus indicate Heaven in the mosaics of the Baptistery
of Ravenna and in the apse of St John Lateran.
The Trees of Jesse and the Trees of Life in early
art are also founded on the acanthus with various symbolical details niched in the branches.
It surrounds the ' Coronation ' and fills the space
above the heads of the saints in the large central
mosaic of S. Maria Maggiore[1] and of the fine
mosaic in S. Clemente.[2] Venturi writes of the
latter:

' From the plant, whence rises the Cross,
spring two green boughs which wreath over all

[1] Rome.   [2] *Ibid.*

Photo Alinari

THE ACANTHUS OF PARADISE
Mosaic of 13th century
(S. Clemente, Rome)

[To face page 146

the abside, enclosing with their spirals birds, flowers and saints to give the idea of the garden of felicity. In such a way, in the *Dugento*, at the distance of so many centuries, the verses of St Paulino da Nola are illustrated once more.'

But after the thirteenth century acanthus plants of vast proportions were no longer used to symbolize the gardens of Heaven. Heaven became a natural park-like place with fruit trees and flower-grown grass, except for its inhabitants, differing little from any princely garden. The plant was still used as the motive of much decoration, ecclesiastical and secular, but it was no longer seen in connection with devotional subjects as the representative plant of Heaven.

XIII

THE FLEUR-DE-LYS

AMONG the symbolical flowers of art, the golden fleurs-de-lys of France hold a high position. They were the arms of the King of France, ' the eldest son of the Church '; they were borne by Saint Louis, the royal saint, and are typical of Christian royalty. Till the reign of Henry VIII they appeared upon the royal banner of England. Their origin, however, in spite of latter-day legends, was non-Christian, nor are they distinctively lilies. The learned M. de Beaumont, who has made a special study of the origins of the fleur-de-lys, or fleur-de-lis, as he prefers to spell it, has thus summed up his researches:

1. Armorial bearings did not commence in France till after the first Crusade.

2. It was in imitation of the Arabs and Persians that chivalry, tourneys and coats of arms were adopted in Europe and France.

3. This flower, which we name the fleur-de-lis, is the symbol of fecundity and royalty in ancient Egypt; it is also the sacred plant and tree of life, adopted with the same symbolical significance by the Assyrians and Persians, from whom it passed to Byzantium, to arrive at last in the Teutonic countries bordering on the East. It came at the same time to the Venetians, and the Lombards, the Spaniards and the French, and this significant form ornamented sceptres and crowns, the attributes of royalty.

4. When the laws of heraldry were at last established in France, after the Crusades, this symbol became the arms of the Kings of France, who entitled themselves *rois par excellence.* Later, the origin being forgotten and lost, the Celtic root of the word *li* was ignored by the heralds. They regarded this symbolical ornament as the *lilium* or garden lily, in itself a symbol of the Virgin, which for the most Christian Kings of France must have been a powerful motive for its adoption. Perhaps even a religious scruple may have been the cause of this transformation of the heathen into the

Christian symbol. It was not till then that the heraldic writers, the greater part of whom belonged to the Church, forced themselves to recognize in the heraldic fleur-de-lys the form of the lilium, even though, in place of being *or* upon *azur* and having three petals, it ought in that case to have five petals and appear in *argent*.[1]

The monkish heralds found a very elaborate symbolism in the royal shield of France. The lilies were of gold, not silver, because in heraldry gold signifies the four kingly virtues, nobility, goodwill, charity and magnanimity.

They are three in number because this number is complete as is the Holy Trinity. . . . Also, the centre one signifies the Christian faith, that on the right the clergy, that on the left the army. There was no end to the hidden meanings.

' *Enfin*,' concludes Carlo Degrassalio of Carcassonne, ' *ces trois fleurs-de-lis d'or sont sur un écu d'azur, parceque, de même que Dieu, le roi des rois, la puissance des puissances, a en quelque*

[1] *Recherches sur l'orgine du Blazon et en particulier la Fleur-de-Lis.*

*sorte pour écu le bleu firmament, resplendissant
d'astres d'or ; de même le roi de France, fils aîné
de l'Eglise, porte pour la plus grande gloire du
Christ, l'écu le plus noble, écu sur lequel les lis
d'or brillent comme les astres sur un ciel serein.'* [1]

Tradition says that the first appearance of
the fleur-de-lys upon this earth was at the
baptism of King Clovis. King Clovis was
married to Clotilda, a Christian Princess of
Burgundy, and her prayers having obtained the
victory for France at a critical moment, he in
gratitude became a Christian also. On the
occasion of his baptism by Saint Rémi an
angel presented him with three heavenly
lilies.

In the Bedford Missal,[2] presented to Henry
VI when he was crowned King of France, the
legend is illustrated in miniature. The angel is
shown receiving the three lilies in Heaven. He
descends to earth and carries them to Saint
Rémi, who reverently receives them in a napkin
and gives them to Queen Clotilda. Lower down
in the picture Clotilda presents the emblazoned

[1] Ragalium Franciæ, Libro duo, 1545.
[2] In possession of Sir J. Tobin.

shield bearing the three fleurs-de-lys to her husband. This legend might seem disproved by the decoration of fleurs-de-lys, which was already upon the great brazen bowl now in the Louvre, known as the Font of King Clovis, had not recent archæological investigation discovered the origin of the bowl to be neither Frankish nor Christian, and the fleurs-de-lys prove merely that the vessel was designed for royal use.

The confusion of the fleur-de-lys with the lily of Heaven and the flower of the Virgin gave it a semi-religious value, which excused its intrusion into the decoration of churches and church furniture. Sometimes it was used entirely heraldically, as the indication of the giver of a gift. It is used heraldically upon the silver shrine of Saint Simeon at Zara, the gift of Louis the Great and his wife, Elizabeth, where the fleur-de-lys of the coat of arms is repeated throughout the entire decoration. Heraldically, yet with some sense of the right placing of the flower which emblemizes purity, were the fleurs-de-lys embroidered with the word *amor* upon the tiny shoes of the *Virgin de los Reyes*. The figure, which is still in Seville Cathedral, was a gift from Saint

Louis of France to his brother saint, Ferdinand of Spain.

The flower is again heraldic upon the magnificent tomb of Robert the Wise,[1] the patron of Giotto and Simone Martini, where it decorates the background with fine effect, though it is perhaps too insistently repeated on crowns, sceptres, brooches and the floriation of crosses; but the constantly-recurring fleurs-de-lys in the architecture of the Cistercian Brotherhood appear quite definitely as the flower of the Virgin. She was the patron of the order, and their famous saint, Bernard of Clairvaux—' her own faithful Bernard '—devoted his life to praising the ' lily of the valley.' Her impress is upon the stone of the Cistercian abbeys of England and of France, where repeatedly we find the ' carved work of open lilies.' But the Cistercians had no monopoly of the symbol. Almost naturally the stone work of French Gothic architecture seems to bud and break into the formal flower. In the great Church of Albi each upspringing slender shaft ends in a *fleur*, alternating with shields along the screen. In the rood-loft of St Floren-

[1] S. Chiara, Naples.

tin, in the town of that name, fleurs-de-lys form the centre of elaborate tracery, and in the rood-loft of the Madeleine at Troyes a very beautiful crowned fleur-de-lys fills the panels of the sur-mounting balustrade.

In the panel [1] designed for the tomb of Edward VI by Torregiano, and now forming part of the altar above Henry VII's tomb, the rose and the lily meet in a charming Renaissance decoration, and the link between the heraldic and the symbolical seems to be supplied, for the personal badges of the king, the Tudor rose and the fleur-de-lys, are woven together in flowing lines, till, losing heraldic stiffness and personal application, they become the Rose of Love and the Lily of Purity, a fit decoration for the altar of God.

But it was not in France and England only that the fleur-de-lys was used as a symbol of royalty. In a Greek miniature of the tenth century [2] fleurs-de-lys are scattered over the mantle of King David, and Didron mentions that he saw a fleur-de-lys ornamentation of the thirteenth century in the Church of Hecatompyli.

[1] Westminster Abbey.
[2] Psalterium cum Figuris, Bib. National.

The miniature was, of course, painted before the lilies had appeared on the royal banner of France, and the decoration at Hecatompyli would be drawn from Eastern sources.

The most noble use of the fleur-de-lys is to express the majesty of God. Floriated crowns as a symbol of Divine majesty were common in French, Flemish and German art, but are seldom seen in Italy. Most usually it is God the Father only who is so distinguished. In a French miniature of the end of the fourteenth century,[1] where the three persons are represented under human form, God the Father wears the floriated crown, the other persons the cruciform halo. In a stained glass window, with the figure of God the Father holding the Crucifix,[2] He wears a tiara of five tiers, each decorated with the fleur-de-lys.

Memling and his school, painting for the Court of Burgundy, held to the French traditions, and God the Father in the ' Coronation ' on the shrine of St Ursula, God the Son in the ' Christ surrounded by Angels ' in Antwerp,

[1] Roman des Trois Pélerinages, Bib. S. Geneviève.
[2] St Martin in Vignes, Troyes.

and the Virgin on the wings (outer) of the ' Last Judgment ' at Danzig, all wear crowns ornamented with fleurs-de-lys.

In German art there are fewer crowns bearing the fleur-de-lys, the crowns of both the Deity and the Virgin having usually the arched imperial form. But very frequently towards the end of the fifteenth century the rays of light, which in Italian art make a cruciform bar across the halo of the Saviour, in Germany take the form of fleurs-de-lys. They are particularly noticeable in ' The Virgin and Saint Anne with the Child ' of Hans Fries,[1] and in a rather more elaborate form in the work of Wolgemut.[2]

There are two saints who have always had the right to wear the royal lilies of France.

They are Saint Louis of France, in his lifetime Louis IX, and his grand-nephew Louis, Bishop of Toulouse.

King Louis, the saintly soldier who brought to France the Crown of Thorns and, to enshrine it, built the Sainte Chapelle, died in Crusade before the walls of Tunis in 1270.

[1] Germanisches Museum, Nuremburg.
[2] Scenes from the Passion, Alte Pinakothek, Munich.

Twenty-seven years later he was canonized, and Giotto painted his portrait in Santa Croce.

Mr Gardner comments on this fresco:

'St Louis the King (one whom Dante does not seem to have held in honour), a splendid figure, calm and noble, in one hand the sceptre and in the other the Franciscan cord, his royal robe besprinkled with the golden lily of France over the armour of the warrior of the Cross, his face absorbed in celestial contemplation. He is the Christian realization of the Platonic philosopher king; "St Louis," says Walter Pater, " precisely because his whole being was full of heavenly vision, in self-banishment from it for a while, led and ruled the French people so magnanimously alike in peace and war." Opposite him is St Louis of Toulouse, with the royal crown at his feet; below are St Elizabeth of Hungary, with her lap full of flowers, and, opposite to her, St Clare, of whom Dante's Piccarda tells so sweetly in the *Paradiso*—that lady on high whom, " perfected life and lofty merit doth enheaven.' "[1] Saint Clare carries a lily.

In the Prado there is a Holy Trinity by C.

[1] Edmund G. Gardner, Florence.

Coello, where Saint Louis is placed opposite to
Saint Elizabeth of Hungary, who holds a basket
of roses, and this grouping of the two royal saints
is often found.   St Elizabeth was canonized
before St Louis was born, but they are well
matched in piety, both of noble birth, both
dying in the flower of their age, and both devoted to their people's welfare.   There is a very
interesting figure of Saint Louis, intellectual,
earnest and strong, in the *Mariage Mystique* [1]
of Jean Perréal.

Saint Louis of Toulouse was the grandson of
Charles of Anjou, who was suzerain of Florence
for ten years.   Perugia chose him as her patron
saint, and in Florence he was patron of the
Parte Guelfa.   He is easily recognized by his
mitre and the fleurs-de-lys upon his cope.
There is a statue of him by Donatello at
Santa Croce, and pictures elsewhere by Bonfigli,
Simone Martini, Moretto and Cosimo Rosselli.

Perhaps the most sympathetic and individual portrait of him is that of Bartolommeo
Vivarini.[2]   He carries book and crozier and his
youthful face is very sweet and earnest, though

----

[1] Louvre.   [2] Uffizi, Florence.

it has the set lips of the true churchman. The
cope is bordered with a large design of fleurs-de-
lys.

Both these saints wear the fleur-de-lys to
mark that they are members of the Royal House
of France. The purity which the lily symbolizes when regarded as the flower of the Virgin
is a secondary significance. Now another holy
one has joined them, who also, though of lowly
birth, bore the golden lilies. But for her they
were the true lilies of maidenhood, their form
merely showing that the right to carry them
on her banner was the gift of a French
king.

'With a wreath woven by no mortal hand shall
she (Jeanne d'Arc) at Reims engarland happily
the gardener of the Lily, named Charles, son of
Charles,' prophesied Engélinde, the Hungarian
seer, and at the fulfilment Charles was not un-
grateful. Since a woman cannot heraldically
bear arms, he granted to the brothers of the maid
the right to wear two of the royal lilies on their
shield. The blazon was *d'azur à la couronne
royale d'or soutenue d'une épée d'argent croisée et
pommetée d'or en pal, cotoyée de deux fleurs-de-lis*

d'or. They were given at the same time (December 1429) the surname of *du lis.*

The sword has the blade ornamented with five fleurs-de-lys and is apparently the famous one unearthed in the Church of St Catharine at Fierbois, 'decked with five flower-de-luces on each side.'[1] But in the least doubtful of the many contemporary portraits of the Maid (those in the collection of M. George Spetz) the fleurs-de-lys do not appear. When questioned at her trial as to any supernatural power held by her sword, she declared: 'It was a rusty sword in the earth, with five crosses on it, and I knew it through my voices.'[2]

The clergy of the Church of St Catharine, however, after finding the sword by Jeanne's directions, had had a scabbard made for it of crimson velvet, embroidered with fleurs-de-lys in gold, and legend supported by heraldry seems to have substituted the fleurs-de-lys of the scabbard for the five crosses of the blade.

The device upon the banner was dictated to her by her patron saints, Margaret and Catharine.

---

[1] First part of *King Henry VI*, Act I. sc. ii.
[2] Trial of Jeanne d'Arc, 1431.

It was of white linen, fringed with silk, and embroidered with a figure of the Saviour holding a globe in His hands, while an angel knelt on either side in adoration. *Jhesus Maria* was inscribed at the foot.   A repetition of this banner recopied from age to age is said to be preserved at Tours.

L

XIV

THE LILY OF THE ANNUNCIATION

THERE is one incident in the life of the Virgin Mary which is particularly associated with lilies. It is the Annunciation.

The Annunciation was not often depicted before the twelfth century, though there are instances of it on some early ivories, on a sarcophagus at Ravenna of the fifth century, in the famous sixth - century Syrian MS. of the Laurentian Library,[1] and among the mosaics of Santa Maria Maggiore.[2] During the twelfth and thirteenth centuries, while the veneration of the Virgin within the Catholic Church steadily grew greater, the story of her life, as apart from that of her Divine Son, appeared in sculpture and stained glass, but still the Annunciation was a comparatively rare subject and simply treated. Early in the fourteenth century, however, a whole flight of announcing angels

[1] Florence.　　　　[2] Rome.

162

settled down over Italy, some drifting as far north as Holland. We find them kneeling, standing, just alighting, often with the wind of swift movement still in their garments and almost always on the left hand of the picture, with the Virgin in the place of honour on the right. The Annunciation, the announcing of the near approach of ' the dayspring from on high,' which was to bring light and joy and freedom to a world groping in the twilight of an imperfect revelation, was an incident which particularly appealed to minds rejoicing in the intellectual liberation of the Renaissance. It appealed, too, to the joyous nature of the Florentines, who hated the sad and tragic aspects of life, loving fresh and spring-like things and rather elaborate simplicity. Pictures of the Annunciation multiplied, particularly in Florence, which was just then evolving the school which was to influence so powerfully the Western world's pictorial conceptions of the divine mysteries. And in the great majority of Annunciations we find lilies, for in this incident of the Virgin's life above all others it was necessary to emphasize the purity which made the wonder of the angel's salutation.

The most characteristic treatment of the lily, as the lily of the Annunciation, was to place it in a pot or vase. About the year 1291, Cavallini, the mosaicist, was in Rome decorating the Church of S. Maria in Trastevere, and beneath the great centre mosaic of the apse he placed a series of scenes from the life of the Virgin. In the Annunciation the Virgin is seated on a marble throne, which has broad, table-like arms. On one arm there is a dish, apparently of fruit, and on the other a vase filled with lilies. The vase may or may not have been placed there definitely as a symbol, but as a detail—in vulgar English phraseology—it caught on. We find it on the famous carved candlestick of Gaeta,[1] worked by an unknown contemporary of Niccola d'Apulia. It appears on an embroidered book-cover of English work [2] attributed to the end of the thirteenth century, and is cleverly squared out of the chequered background of a Netherlandish music-book [3] of 1330.

The vase of lilies soon became a more or less elaborate detail in numerous illuminations,

---

[1] At Gaeta.   British Museum.
[3] South Kensington Museum.

carvings and paintings. The earliest of the Flemish masters, Jan van Eyck,[1] Roger van der Weyden[2] and the Master of Flémalle,[3] make use of it. It was particularly popular in Florence. The Florentines loved the Annunciation as a subject and were charmed by the easy, graceful symbolism of the lilies. They were also, doubtless, deeply gratified, as citizens and as churchmen, to identify the lily, their city's badge, as the flower of the Virgin.

In Spain, even before there was any native school of painting, the vase of lilies passed from being a detail to be an almost essential factor in every representation of the Annunciation, and early in the fifteenth century we find it standing detached as the special and distinguishing attribute of the Virgin. In the insignia of the Order of the Lily of Aragon, founded in 1410 by Ferdinand, Duke of Pegnafiel, the chain was composed of alternate griffins and pots of three lilies, and Ford mentions that when the Regent Fernando recovered Antequera from the Moors he gave the city for arms the badge of his

[1] Imperial Gallery, St Petersburg.
[2] Alte Pinakothek, Munich.   [3] Collection Mérode, Brussels.

military order, which was *La Terraza,* ' the vase,' the pot of lilies of the Virgin.[1]

The symbol of the vase had come to the Netherlands and Germany while they were still pictorially inarticulate; but when they at length found means of expression, the Germans slowly, the Flemings in a splendid burst with the van Eycks, it was their earliest and their favourite symbol. Memling places it also beside his enthroned Madonnas, and it is never omitted from an Annunciation except on the occasions, comparatively rare in the North, when Gabriel holds a branch of lilies in his hand instead of the herald's wand. Then there is no vase, for there is no necessity to repeat the symbol.

But in Italy itself the vase of lilies, though popular, was never considered essential. No vase decorates the loggias where sit the Virgins of Giotto,[2] Botticelli,[3] Melozzo da Forlì,[4] or Leonardo da Vinci,[5] though Giotto introduces it with identical symbolism in the Visitation. Indeed many of the most typical painters of

---

[1] *Spanish Handbook*, first edition.
[2] Lower Church, Assisi.   [3] Uffizi, Florence.
[4] Pantheon, Rome.   [5] Uffizi, Florence.

both the early and the high Renaissance, Taddeo di Bartolo,[1] Spinello Aretino,[2] Fra Angelico,[3] Lorenzo di Credi[4] and Raphael,[5] banish lilies entirely, both from the vase and from the angel's hand. Ghirlandaio places a vase beside the Virgin's reading-desk, but alters its significance by filling it with roses, daisies and jasmine, the flowers of love, innocence and divine hope.[6]

On the other hand, some of the Florentine artists who had a special fondness for the flower, notably Fra Filippo Lippi,[7] and the Della Robbias,[8] use both, so doubling the symbolism; but it was more correct, where there was a vase of lilies, to show the angel with folded hands or with a branch of olive, or, as in the beautiful Annunciation of Jan van Eyck at St Petersburg, holding the herald's wand. In Jan van Eyck's Annunciation at Berlin, where Gabriel carries a magnificent bunch of lilies, there is no vase.

According to Northern tradition the true Annunciation lily should have no stamens, but this was a refinement of symbolism largely

[1] Belle Arti, Siena.
[2] SS. Annunziata, Arezzo.
[3] Museo di S. Marco, Florence.
[4] Uffizi, Florence.
[5] Vatican, Rome.
[6] Cathedral, S. Giminiano.
[7] National Gallery.
[8] Spedale degli Innocenti, Florence.

ignored by artists, who were discouraged probably by the insipid appearance of the flower when
deprived of its gold-dusted centre. In Italy it
was entirely neglected, but some painters of the
sixteenth century have placed a tiny flame in the
centre of each lily-cup; a burning flame, according to Vasari,[1] signifying eternal love.

There seems to have been sometimes a doubt
in the minds of the Northern artists as to which
was really the Madonna's flower, the *lilium
candidum* or the iris, which so closely resembled
in form the golden lilies on the royal shields of
France and England.

Memling, who had painted the fleur-de-lys
heraldically for the Duke of Burgundy,[2] seemed
unable to decide, and in the vase of the Annunciation,[3] as well as in the vase which stands beside the enthroned Madonna,[4] he has placed an
iris among the white lilies. Or possibly, with a
deeper symbolism, taking the iris as the fleur-
de-lys, the ancient symbol of royalty, which,
with its three united petals, recalls also the

[1] *Lives of the Painters*, Titian.
[2] Diptych of Jeanne de Bourbon, Musée Condé, Chantilly.
[3] Collection of Prince U. Radziwill, Berlin.
[4] Royal Gallery, Berlin.

Pinturicchio   *Photo Alinari*

THE ROSE OF DIVINE LOVE RISING FROM A PRECIOUS VESSEL
(Borgia Apartment, Vatican)

Pesello   *Photo Alinari*

THE ROYAL LILY SPRINGING FROM A HUMBLE VASE
(S. Spirito, Florence)

To face page 169

nature of the Holy Trinity, he has striven to interpret florally the message of the angel, that God incarnate would spring from a lily-like virginity. It may not be without design that the iris in the Annunciation is overshadowed by the lilies, while in the picture where the Holy Child sits upon His Mother's lap, the iris in the vase (in this case marked with the sacred monogram) has sprung upwards beyond the white lilies.

In the Church of S. Spirito in Florence there is an altar-piece of the Annunciation which was at one time attributed to Botticelli and is now usually ascribed to Pesello. The vase, placed midway between the two figures, holds three purple irises. Perhaps the artist saw a symbol of the Holy Trinity in the three royal lilies growing on one stalk (though the Church held a belief in the incarnation of the Trinity in unity to be heresy), in which case the colour, the purple of humility, would be appropriate.

More difficult to explain is the symbolism of the vase of lilies in the Annunciation upon the cover of a psalter, in fine English needlework

of the thirteenth century.[1] The book belonged
to Anne, daughter of Sir Simon Felbrigge, and
if the date given, the end of the thirteenth
century, is correct, it is a very early instance of
the Virgin's vase of lilies. The figures have
much dignity and sweep of line, but the lily,
which is a fleur-de-lys in form, is red! Possibly
in the garden of the country convent where em-
broidery was worked no liliums grew. The nun
would therefore take the only lilies she knew,
those of the royal standard. For colour she
would remember that they surpassed Solomon
in his glory. But, even so, the red lily argues an
insensitiveness to symbolic values scarcely to
be found among the Latins.

The original symbolism of the vase of lilies
was simple. It signified the purity of the Maid
of Nazareth, she of whom it was prophesied ' A
Virgin shall conceive and bear a Son.' She
does not hold the flower in her hand as do
the virgin martyrs who preserved their purity
through storm and stress, but it grows naturally
beside her and merely typifies her girlhood. In
the first half of the fifteenth century this seems

[1] British Museum.

to have been the invariable intention. But in the later half of that century the meaning was developed and amplified. Distinction was made between the vase and the flower it contained. In France and in Spain, where religious iconography is found in architectural detail rather than in pictorial decoration, the favourite arrangement of the Annunciation was to place the vase midway between the Virgin and the angel, a composition which from its equal balance was most decorative. The Virgin with drooping head and falling veil, Gabriel with curved wings, both leaning forward towards the central vase of lilies, formed an ideal filling for a lunette or the spandrels of an arch, and the simplicity of the group made it particularly suitable for sculpture, both in wood and stone. It is the central motive of many of the great carved and gilded reredos in Spain and of the simpler stone altars of France. The central vase of lilies had, however, a tendency to become ever larger, till, from being a detail, it became the important centre-point, and in some French Annunciations of the sixteenth century the uninstructed heathen would merely see two figures worshipping, apparently, a large vase of flowers.

In two Italian pictures, that of doubtful origin already mentioned which is in S. Spirito, and the Annunciation of Pinturicchio in the Vatican, where the large vase is placed exactly in the centre of the composition, the flowers within the vase are not white lilies; they are iris, the royal lily, in one case, and roses, the flower of divine love, in the other. Therefore the flower-filled vase was no longer strictly the symbol of the Virgin's purity. A change, hinted at when Memling placed the iris among the lilies, had come about, for the flower which was the attribute of Jesus Christ was now rising from the vase and distinction had been made between the vase and the flower which it contained. Christ is the mystic flower springing from a lowly vessel. He is the flower, Mary the vase. The royal purple lily or the rose of love are, therefore, as appropriate a filling for the vase as was the lily, and there is no incongruity in any attitude of homage towards the vase on the part of the Virgin. But since the compound emblem was the emblem of the Immaculate Conception,.

naturally it is most often the lily of purity which fills the vase.

In the Annunciation of Albert Dürer's ' Smaller Passion ' [1] the lily growing in its humble earthen pot undeniably refers to the perfect sinlessness of the soul which was yet to be born, for the flowers are still each tightly folded in its bud, while in the culminating scene of the series, where the Saviour sits in judgment, the lily, with each calyx fully expanded, is shown with the sword of justice behind His head.

Northern symbolism, always deeper and more complicated than that of the South, required that the vase which contained the lilies should be transparent, thus indicating the perfect purity of the body which enshrined the soul of perfect innocence. ' In so far that the glass allows all surroundings to shine through without being itself harmed, it has become the symbol of the Immaculate Conception. Therefore in pictures of the Annunciation a blossoming lily stalk in a transparent glass is placed at the feet of the Virgin.' [2]

---

[1] British Museum. [2] W. Menzel, *Christliche Symbolik*.

The same idea is traced in the thirteenth-
century Christmas carol:

> ' As the sunbeam through the glass
> Passeth but not staineth,
> So the Virgin as she was,
> Virgin still remaineth.' [1]

And somewhat akin is the mirror which occasionally appears, held by an attendant *putto* in a
Spanish ' Immaculate Conception.'

The transparent vase is not often seen in
Italian Annunciations, for it was usual in Italy
to place the stalk of lilies, a complete symbol in
itself of virginity, in the angel's hand, and there
was no need to double the symbolism; but the
painters of the late fifteenth and early sixteenth
centuries, in pictures of Mary with the Child or
in a Holy Family, use the crystal vase frequently as an attribute of the Infant Saviour,
filling it with those flowers which express His
virtues, the violet of humility, the rose or carnation of divine love, the daisy of innocence, or
the jasmine of heavenly hope. [2]

[1] *Dies in lætitiæ*, Neale's translation.
[2] The large transparent vase which stands beside the
Madonna with the Child, by Jean Perréal, in the Louvre, contains iris, the white lily, lily of the valley and columbine.

The actual number of blooms upon the lily stalk has also its significance. Some think they should be three in number, two fully opened flowers and one in bud, forming what Rossetti terms the ' Tripoint.'

> ' I' the centre is the Tripoint: perfect each
> Except the second of its points, to teach
> That Christ is not yet born.'

Several of the masters of the fourteenth and fifteenth centuries painted the two flowers with the bud or three fully-opened blooms, but more often, arguing possibly that this lily was the emblem of God the Son when made Man, and not of the Holy Trinity, they painted simply a natural lily plant with clustering buds and one or many blossoms, taking the whole plant as the symbol.

Sometimes the vase holds three distinct stalks of lilies with a single bloom on each, an arrangement which was suggested, it is said, by the Dominican legend of the doubting Master.

A Master of the Dominicans, unable to believe in the stainlessness of the Blessed Virgin, went to ask help of the saintly brother Egidius.

' O Master of the Preachers,' said Egidius,

on meeting him, ' Virgo ante partum.' He struck the ground with his staff and from the spot there immediately sprang a lily. ' O doubting Master,' he said again, ' Virgo in partu.' He struck the earth and again a lily sprang. He spoke a third time, ' O my brother, Virgo post partum,' a third lily bloomed, and the Master of the Dominicans doubted no more.

A detached vase holding three lily blooms occurs frequently as the motive of an architectural decoration executed in low relief, one beautiful example being above the door of the Badia Church of Florence. But it is not confined to buildings of Dominican origin, and the arrangement seems to owe its popularity more to its symmetry than to any supporting legend. In pictures, where greater freedom of treatment is desirable, the lilies are one, two, three or more —there is no rule.

XV

THE LILY OF THE ANGEL GABRIEL

IN the majority of the Annunciations which were painted during the fourteenth and fifteenth centuries the archangel Gabriel carries a lily. In the earliest representations of the subject he has simply a herald's wand, which in later Byzantine art usually terminated in a fleur-de-lys, the ancient symbol of royalty, or in a more or less elaborate cross. More rarely he carries a scroll on which are inscribed the words of his message.

In the early Sienese school he still holds the herald's wand,[1] or brings to the Virgin a branch of olive,[2] the symbol of peace and goodwill. Once at least he holds a branch of laurel,[3] the meed of those who excel, and sometimes the palm[4] of victory over sin.

[1] Duccio di Buoninsegna, National Gallery.
[2] Giovanni di Paolo, Vatican.
[3] Andrea Vanni, Collection Saracini, Siena.
[4] Ambrogio Lorenzetti, Belle Arti, Siena.

In the famous Annunciation of Simone
Martini,[1] Gabriel, who carries a branch of olive,
is also olive-crowned, and this seems to be the
proper symbolism of the subject. The messenger
of God, crowned with peace, brings the olive
branch of reconciliation between God and man
to the Virgin, beside whom stands a vase filled
with the lilies which symbolize her purity. The
dove hovers above.

It has not been decided which artist was the
first to place the stalk of lilies in the angel
Gabriel's hand, and first had come the lovely
symbol of the vase of lilies by the Virgin's side.
But in the Annunciation, which forms part of
Simone Martini's polyptych in the Museum of
Antwerp, we find the herald's wand just turning
to a lily. Professor A. Venturi, in his magnificent
History of Italian Art, describes it. The angel
' holds a lily with a long stem, which is all white.
Thus the stick or sceptre of ivory, which we have
already seen in Duccio's picture, has become
partly stick, partly lily-stem. With Duccio it is
still the sceptre with three points, that Gabriel,
messenger of God, holds as sign of authority.

[1] Uffizi, Florence.

But look how the three points change themselves to lily-buds, and open the corolla, as the archangel extends the candid flower towards the Virgin, who was saluted by David and the Fathers as " The lily of the valleys.'' The poetry of Christian art thus overthrows mediæval materialism and lavishes flowers on fair likenesses of Mary.'

In this Annunciation we find the three types of lilies used in art—the lily growing freely and naturally in a vase beside the Virgin; the stiff lily, half conventionalized in the angel's hand; and the fleurs-de-lys, wholly conventional, which ornament the arms of the Virgin's seat.

Simone Martini died in 1344, and by 1359, the date of its completion, every Florentine artist must have seen the wonderful tabernacle raised by Orcagna in Or San Michele, and every artist in Italy must have heard descriptions of the shrine.

' Che passa di bellezza, s'io ben recolo,
Tutti gli altri che son dentro del secolo.' ¹

On a panel of the Tabernacle there is an Annunciation which was the most beautiful

¹ Sacchetti.

representation of the subject so far given to the world, and the kneeling angel with the sweeping wings carries in his left hand a heavy stalk of *lilium candidum*.

It is interesting to trace the evolution of the straight smooth stick which the angel held in the earliest representations of the Annunciation into the natural branch of lilies carried by the typical Announcing Angel of Christian art. First we find upon the wand the three-pointed fleur-de-lys, which from the days of the Assyrians had ornamented the royal sceptre. The heavenly herald bore a wand ornamented with the royal symbol when he brought a message from the Lord of the Universe to the Maiden of the House of David, who was to be the Mother of His Son. Gradually the fleur-de-lys gained some likeness to the natural lily. The sceptre was made of ivory. It was white. Two leaves appeared wreathing the stick. Midway in the transformation are the lilies carried by the lovely choir of seated angels in a picture by Guariento.' Each angel holds in his left hand an orb and in the right a straight lily stem with

' Museum of Padua.

leaves growing naturally up its whole length. At the top is a single flower, which, seen in profile, has the shape of the fleur-de-lys. Simone Martini indicates the blossom's cup-like form. With Orcagna we find the fully-realized stem of lilies. One unidentified master of the fourteenth century [1] went even further in botanical fidelity, and paints the bulb and pendent rootlets, though, strangely enough, he at the same time keeps to the old convention and places a scroll in the hand of both Madonna and angel.

Meanwhile, in 1344, Ambrogio di Lorenzetti had painted an Annunciation [2] in which the angel, crowned with olive, holds the palm branch with which the ancient Romans were accustomed to salute a conqueror. The symbol of the palm was used also by Spinello Aretino,[3] a pupil of Giotto, and was supported by Dante, who describes the angel Gabriel as:

> ' He that bore the palm
> Down unto Mary, when the Son of God
> Vouchsafed to clothe Him in terrestrial weeds.'

But it did not come into general use in this con-

---

[1] Vatican.   [2] Belle Arti, Siena.

[3] The Cathedral, Arezzo.

nection, and chiefly for the reason that the palm became consecrated to representations of the last scenes of the Virgin's life. The *Legenda Aurea*, when recounting how the angel Gabriel announced to the Virgin her approaching death, states: 'He (Gabriel) gave her a branch of palm from Paradise, which he commanded should be borne before her bier.'

The palm was, therefore, a necessary detail in this scene, and it was probably to avoid confusion between these two separate appearances of the angel to the Virgin that the palm has been reserved entirely for the last Annunciation. The religious sentiment of the age forbade the portrayal of any sign of decrepitude in the Virgin even at the hour of her death, and except for the substitution of the palm for the lily and the reversal of the usual places of the figures, the Virgin being placed on the left and the angel on the right, it would be difficult to distinguish the scene where the Virgin receives the news of her approaching death, from that in which her approaching motherhood is announced to her.

It became the general rule, then, for Gabriel, as the angel of the Annunciation of the Saviour's birth, to carry a lily. But the rule was not invariable. The early Flemish artists, half painters, half craftsmen, loved to depict the delicately-chiselled gold of jewelled sceptres topped by an elaborate fleur-de-lys or the cross-surmounted orb which signified the sovereignty of Christ upon earth. These precious sceptres accorded well with the opulent and prosaic comfort of the surroundings in which they set the sacred drama, and reflect the spirit of the Northern mystics. The clear detailed visions of Saint Matilda, the inspired nun of Saxony, which occurred during the last half of the thirteenth century, and whose imagery has distinctly influenced Northern religious art, fairly scintillate with mystical gems. Even the roses and the lilies, symbols, she tells us, of divine love and innocence, which she saw in her glimpses of Heaven, were embroidered in gold and silver thread upon rich stuffs or cloth of gold.

Italian art had different traditions. It began with the utter simplicity of Giotto and Fra Angelico, though the Byzantine love of rich trappings still lingered in Siena. As Florentine art progressed it did indeed become more elaborate, till its inclination to magnificence was severely checked by Savonarola, whose influence on art has usually been wrongly estimated. He was no blind iconoclast, though without doubt objects of great artistic worth were burnt in his famous holocaust of 'vanities,' which finished the Carnival of 1497. On the contrary, as Senator Pasquale Villari points out, he was always surrounded by the best artists of his century. Fra Bartolommeo, for four years after his death, did not touch a brush, such was his grief. The Della Robbias were devoted to him; two received the habit from his hands. Lorenzo di Credi was his partisan; Cronaca ' would speak of nothing but the things of Savonarola.' Botticelli illustrated his works, and Michael Angelo was a most constant listener to his preaching.

He spoke plainly to the painters from his pulpit. The beauty of the Divinity, of the Virgin and the Saints was the beauty of holiness, not of outward adornment of fine raiment, gold and jewels, and ' the beauty of man or woman in so far as it approaches to the primal beauty, so is it great and more perfect.' [1]

[1] Sermon on Ezekiel.

We read of the Virgin that by her great beauty the men who saw her were astonished (stupefatti).

. . . 'Do you believe that she went about in the manner in which you paint her? I say to you that she went dressed as a poor woman!'' [1]

But he who taught for choice beneath the damask rose in the centre of his cloister admitted roses and lilies where he denounced rubies and pearls. Flowers alone survived as emblems or as votive decoration even after the puritanical current towards the ideal set in motion by the great Dominican became merged in the over-sweeping wave of classicism—and even those late artists who dispensed with every other convention for the expression of the abstract, placed a lily in the angel Gabriel's hand.

Modern art has adopted the tradition and in the 'Ecce Ancilla Domini' of Rossetti [2] the wingless angel carries a stalk of lilies. There is also a white lily embroidered upon the strip of material which is stretched upon an embroidery frame at the foot of Mary's bed.

The angel brings the lily to the Virgin in

---

[1] Sermon on Amos and Zachariah.   [2] Tate Gallery.

recognition of her perfect purity, the transcendent quality by which alone she found favour with God. Through it tremendous honour came upon her, and by the marvellous nature of that honour she was eternally bound to her virginity. ' Mary Virgin, ever a Virgin.' In a very charming picture by Filippo Lippi,[1] Mary, with bent head, and fully understanding the grave significance of the gift, reverently accepts the lily which the angel Gabriel places in her hand.

In another Annunciation by Filippo Lippi,[2] a second angel, peeping through the entry behind Gabriel, also carries a lily, but it is a fancy which seems to have no particular significance and rather impairs the dignity of the subject.

So constantly did painters and sculptors of the Annunciation place a lily in the archangel Gabriel's hand that it gradually became his special attribute, which he wore, as a knight did his crest, to distinguish him from other angels and archangels.

In the apocryphal Book of Tobit is the story of Tobias, who was accompanied by the angel Raphael on the famous journey which he took

[1] In the collection of Miss Hertz, Rome.   [2] Pinakothek, Munich.

to recover his father's money, a journey in which he not only caught the fish whose gall was to cure his father's blindness, but also found a wife. It is the only subject from the Apocrypha which now decorates Christian churches, and owes this grace to the force with which the story, despite its fantastic details, illustrates the constant watchfulness of Heaven over those still on their earthly pilgrimage. In the fifteenth century it was a favourite subject for a votive picture on behalf of one about to take a journey. The young man, rather helpless in his youth and inexperience, protected by the strong, wise guardian angel, was a group painted with the greatest pleasure, and the fascination of ideal, sexless beauty, of curved, sweeping wings, tempted to an amplification of the subject, and though the Book of Tobit mentions one archangel only—

> '. . . . The affable archangel
> Raphael; the sociable spirit that deign'd
> To travel with Tobias, and secured
> His marriage with the seven-times wedded maid—'[1]

there suddenly sprang up in Florence a short-

[1] Milton.

lived fashion for depicting Tobias with three archangels.

There are two of these pictures in Florence;[1] others at Verona,[2] Turin[3] and Munich.[4] In each Michael is armed, Raphael grasps Tobias by the hand, and Gabriel carries a branch of lilies.

But the four figures in a row make an awkward composition, and stiffness is avoided at the expense of dignity. A mincing angel, too conscious of his pretty wings and daintily-held lily, is the Gabriel of the best known of these pictures, attributed of late years to Botticini.

The lily is, of course, here used non-symbolically, merely to distinguish one archangel from another, and for the same reason that Michael is given the sword and frequently the scales for the weighing of souls, Raphael the traveller's staff and gourd, or, when with Tobias, a small box. The angel Gabriel's primary function is to be the herald of God, as it is Michael's to lead the hosts of Heaven, and Raphael's to guide

[1] Botticini, Accademia; School of Botticelli, Accademia.
[2] Carotto, S. Eufemia, Verona.
[3] Alte Pinakothek.
[4] Rossello di Jacopo Franchi, Accademia, Florence.

The Master of Flémalle   *Photo Hanfstängl*

SAINT BARBARA WITH THE ROYAL LILY

(Prado)

Jörg Breu

THE COLUMBINE OF THE SEVEN GIFTS

(Berlin)

[To face page 188

the straying. Therefore Gabriel carries the herald's wand, now developed to a lily, Michael the sword, and Raphael the staff.

Thus Gabriel, when in company with other archangels and angels, carries the lily to establish his identity, but where, as in a Coronation [1] or an Enthroned Madonna, he stands with Saint Michael guarding the throne, he usually holds also a scroll with ' AVE MARIA ' upon it, showing that the main function of the lily is to proclaim the spotlessness of the Virgin.

A rather charming treatment of the Annunciation lily, which originated in Germany, is to strew the lily heads upon the floor. They then have the appearance of having fallen from Heaven in a shower, like those falling roses, symbols of divine love, which were so often painted by the artists of Italy and Spain. ' The Master of the Sterzinger Altar ' [2] introduces seven of these lily blooms and buds, snapped off short, and with only an inch or two of stalk, into his fine Annunciation painted in 1458, and, satisfied with these, he uses lilies neither in a vase nor in the angel's hand. Other artists of his day

[1] Luca Signorelli.   [2] Rathaus, Sterzing.

liked the fancy well, but wished to keep the mystic vase, so, to avoid doubling the symbol, they turned the fallen flowers to roses, or roses and carnations, symbols of the divine favour which had fallen upon the maid. It was a graceful exposition of the underlying meaning of the scene, symbolically right and delightful in pictorial effect.

XVI

THE FLOWERS OF THE DIVINITY

THE only growing thing which is used to represent the Trinity in Unity is the trefoil or shamrock. Saint Patrick is said to have plucked
from the ground a leaf of shamrock and by it
illustrated to the heathen Irish the mystery of
the Triune Godhead.   Architectural details, and
more especially windows, based upon the trefoil's
form, are common in Gothic churches. In
pictorial art it is rather unusual as an emblem,
but Michael Angelo, who so rarely used symbolical detail, paints the triple-leaved plant
and no other leaf or flower in the foreground
of his Holy Family.[1]

But though the trefoil is the only direct
floral emblem of the Trinity, distinct reference
to it is often found in the triple grouping of the
flowers which are the attributes of the Saviour.
For instance, the three carnations of divine love

[1] Uffizi.

in the crystal vase before the Infant Christ in
Hugo van der Goes' 'Adoration of the Shepherds';[1] the three lilies (one in bud) which the
angel holds in Crivelli's 'Annunciation';[2] and
the three irises in the Annunciation of Pesello.[3]

There is no plant or flower used as the emblem of God the Father. From time to time
the Hebrew metaphor of the Burning Bush has
been used pictorially to indicate His presence;
but as early as the fifth century this image was
appropriated to express the purity of the Virgin
Mother, enveloped but not consumed by the
divine love.

In the Catacombs and on many mediæval
crucifixes the Person of God the Father is indicated by a hand issuing from the clouds and
holding a wreath of laurel, palm or olive. But
the wreath in this case is not the attribute of
the Divine Father, but the attribute of him
above whose head the wreath is held. In the
Catacombs it is the martyr's crown; on the
crucifix it is Christ's crown of victory over sin.

As already mentioned, the lily of purity and
the olive branch of peace are occasionally used

[1] Uffizi.   [2] Frankfort-on-Maine.   [3] S. Spirito, Florence.

as the attributes of God the Holy Ghost. As His direct emblem the dove only is employed, since Scripture states that He descended in ' the form of a dove.' Sometimes in French manuscripts of the fourteenth century He is represented in human form, but such representations are seldom found elsewhere.

Poetry and art have enwreathed the entire life of Jesus Christ with flowers.

' The Annunciation was the festival of early spring. Christ, whose birth was foretold by Gabriel, was a flower that blossomed from the stem of Jesse; His Mother, to whom the imagery of the Song of Solomon was applied, was a flower of the fields and a " lily of the valley." And the place where the Annunciation occurred had a name, Nazareth, which in Hebrew, according to an old but incorrect interpretation, means flower. Such a meeting of associations was naturally not left unutilized by the theological authors. It was often set forth in sermons how the promise of the birth of God as man was connected with the spring's promise of flowers and fruit. S. Bernard in particular worked out the flower symbolism of the Annunciation in poetic

N

and ingenious conceits. The flower, he said, had been willing, at the time of flowering, to be born of a flower in a flower—*i.e.*, Jesus permitted Himself to be announced to Mary at Nazareth in the spring: " Flos nasci voluit de flore, in flore, et floris tempore.' " [1]

So we find a stem of lilies or a vase of flowers as the symbol of His miraculous birth, and on the morning of His nativity rejoicing angels carried olive branches as they sang of peace on earth and goodwill towards men. A helpless Infant, He lay upon the ground to receive the Adoration of His Mother and of angels, among roses of love and lilies of purity, or in grass thick with the daisies, violets and strawberries which told of His innocence, humility and righteousness.

As a boy, growing perhaps to a consciousness of His mission, in Spain He is found with thorny roses, wounding Himself sometimes with the thorns of grief and suffering springing from His divine love itself.

Early devotional art left Christ's life with its miracles and parables and passed to His Passion.

[1] Yrjö Hirn, *The Sacred Shrine.*

For the entry into Jerusalem there is the palm of victory and the olive branch of peace. In the Ecce Homo He wears the Crown of Thorns, and the reed as a sceptre is placed in His hand. For the Crucifixion Signorelli painted below the Cross many pleasant flowers, among which are noticeable the violet and daisy. But the Northern schools reserved for this scene the bitter herbs and flowers, the willow, dandelion and thistle. These weeds, carefully chosen and painted with marvellous minuteness, fill the fore-ground in the Crucifixion by an unnamed German master in the National Gallery.

In the last scenes of all of the divine tragedy there is no symbol but the Crown of Thorns, and to the Resurrection no flower is specially dedicated. But in the Thomas Altar,[1] by the Master of the Bartholomew Altar, the newly-risen Christ is shown, and round His feet, upon the marble step, are lying blossoms of violets and daisies and seven heads of the holy columbine.

The passion flower does not appear in art before the seventeenth century. It was un-known in Europe before the Spanish conquest

[1] Wallraf Richartz Museum, Cologne.

of South America, and it is said that when the
Jesuits brought home reports of the miraculous
flower bearing the insignia of the Passion, which
grew from tree to tree in the forests of the new
land, their tale was first received as a pious invention. But the plant itself at length arrived,
and early in the eighteenth century Francesco
Trevisani painted a delightful little picture [1] less
noticed than it deserves to be. The Virgin, who
is very sweet and gentle, both in pose and expression, sits sewing beside a table on which
is a vase of roses and lilies. The little Christ,
who has apparently just run in from the garden,
points out to His Mother, with a most childlike
gesture, the little thorny crown upon the passion
flower which He holds in His hand. The picture,
which is not unlike the work of Andrea del Sarto
in miniature, is wonderfully attractive.

[1] Uffizi.

XVII

THE FLOWERS OF THE VIRGIN

THERE were many flowers used by the early writers as similes of the Virgin.

> ' Thou art the myrtle and the blooming rose of Paradise,
> Thou art the fairness of heaven, and
> The feast-day of our hearts,'

wrote Saint Petrus Damiani in the eleventh century.

In Saint Bernard we read:

' Mary is the violet of humility, the lily of chastity and the rose of charity.'

Conrad von Würtzburg compares her to the balsam of purest perfume, the fairest among flowers, the cedar of Lebanon, the cypress of Zion, fennel and mint, the white lily, the early flowering almond, the healing mandrake, the musk-flower, the evergreen myrtle, the low nard, the thornless rose in the dew of heaven, the noble frankincense and the hidden violet, and further addresses her as

> ' A living Paradise
> Of grandly coloured flowers.' [1]

But though poets, and particularly German poets, ranged widely through the fields in their search for blossoms which by their beauty or by their healing virtues were fit to symbolize the Virgin, the early artists painted very few. In those mystical Enclosed Gardens which so charmed the Germans of the fifteenth century, only a few plants appear. The lily, which is often the lily of the valley, the rose, the violet, and the strawberry, are the most usual. Later the iris, the royal lily, was added, and sometimes the seven-blossomed columbine. Occasionally in Italy the jasmine and the daisy are also found in the vase beside her, but all other flowers of the garden and field, the tulip, anemone, ranunculus, primrose, daffodil, dahlia, etc., were rigidly excluded.

It will be noticed that, with the exception of the rose, all the flowers of the Virgin are white

[1] *Goldene Schmiede.*

or blue, her own colours. An exception, which is unique, is the golden sunflower springing from her halo on a twelfth-century window in the Church of St Rémi at Reims, and even that is not exclusively hers, since Saint John, on the other side, bears the same flower. White and blue are the two colours which are held most sacred in the Christian Church. White, symbol of the Supreme Being and of the Eternal Truth, is used in the ornaments for the feast of Our Lord and of the Virgin, for it announces loving-kindness, virginity and charity.[1] Blue is the symbol of chastity, innocence and candour. Only one yellow flower is used symbolically, and that only in scenes from the Passion, by artists of the early Flemish and German schools. It is the dandelion, and its significance is, apparently, bitterness of grief.

The white lily, which symbolizes purity, is found chiefly in pictures of the Annunciation, but it has been introduced in many other scenes from the life of the Virgin. In the first exhibited painting by Rossetti, entitled 'The Girlhood of Mary Virgin,'[2] the Virgin, in grey robes, is

[1] Huysman, *La Cathédrale.*   [2] Collection of Lady Jekyll.

seated at a curiously-shaped frame embroidering
a white lily upon a ground of red material. The
flower she is copying grows in a vase beside her
and an angel with rose-coloured wings waters
it. St Anne stands near, and in the background
Joachim trims a trellised vine upon which the
Holy Dove is perched. In the ' Ecce Ancilla
Domini '[1] of Rossetti, this same strip of em-
broidery, now finished, hangs beside the bed.

The older artists paint no lily in the early
scenes of the Virgin's life; it first appears at the
Annunciation, where it was used so repeatedly
that it became in itself the symbol of the miraculous birth of Our Lord. Giotto brings it forward
in the ' Visitation.'[2]   Elizabeth, hurrying from
the house to meet the Virgin, passes beneath a
portico on which blooms a large vase of lilies.

There are endless pictures representing the
Virgin seated with the Holy Child, in which a
vase of lilies is placed as a votive offering before
her feet, or lilies are held by attendant angels.
One of the earliest of these pictures is the
' Enthroned Madonna '[3] of Giotto.   Two angels

---

[1] Tate Gallery, London.   [2] Lower Church, Assisi.
[3] Accademia, Florence.

offer golden vases filled with lilies and roses. The angels have searched Paradise for its most precious flowers and have chosen those which symbolize purity and divine love. As the symbol of divine love the roses are very appropriately mixed with the lilies in the vase which Ghirlandaio[1] places on the lowest step of the Madonna's throne. He has also added the starry wild white campion which closely resembles jasmine, a flower never definitely accorded to the Queen of Heaven by the symbolists of the Church, but its clear starlike form bringing to mind both her title *Stella Maris* and the starry crown described by Saint John, painters frequently use it, and white flowers of the same shape, as her attribute.

But the appearance of the jasmine in the Madonna pictures may in part be owing to some confusion between the jasmine and the myrtle, for the latter was quite definitely one of the Virgin's flowers and is even used when addressing her in metaphor.

> ' O myrtle tree of Paradise
> So richly hung with fruit.' [2]

---

[1] Uffizi, Florence.   [2] *Goldene Schmiede.*

Dr Anselm Saltzer, O.S.B., writes: ' The Greeks and Romans held the myrtle to be the symbol of beauty, youth and marriage, because of its delightful perfume, its evergreen leaves, white blossoms and aromatic berries. In connection with Mary, the myrtle serves as a figure of her purity and other virtues as well as of her influence over the unruly impulses of the human soul.' [1]

Francesco Franciabigio [2] places a vase of single white roses at the Virgin's feet. Double roses, pink or red, are the symbol of divine love, the love of Christ for His Church upon earth, and the white single roses might be the symbol of the passionless love of the ' Mater Consolatrix.'

These flowers, placed in vases before the Virgin, are usually significant and appropriate, but they are really more votive than symbolical. The Latins had brought to the shrine of Venus the myrtle and roses, the apples and poppies that were sacred to her, and painters of Central Italy in the fourteenth and fifteenth centuries,

[1] *Die Sinnbilder und Beiworte Mariens in der deutschen Literatur und lateinischen Hymnenpoesie des Mittelalters.*
[2] Uffizi, Florence.

with the same desire to present and sacrifice to their Lady the flowers which were by association peculiarly hers, painted roses and lilies carefully and beautifully in the foreground of her pictures. It was their gift to the Madonna, as the paper roses on so many modern altars and the wild flowers on the wayside shrines are also gifts.

In Northern Italy, particularly among those who studied in the school of Squarcione, fruit took the place of the votive flowers, and is laid before the Madonna and the Child, or hung in garlands across the upper part of the picture.

The painters of the Italian Renaissance, in spite of diligent classical study, were probably quite unconscious of this survival of paganism in their work. But the ancient traditions of the soil did crop up from time to time, in the same way that traces of the Norse conception of Heaven as a magnificent big-game hunt appear occasionally beneath the symbolism of Christian mediæval art in Germany.

North of the Alps, where the pre-Christian sacrifices had usually run with blood, there was no inherited love of floral offerings, and we seldom find these votive vases or wreaths.

The Madonna attributed to Mabuse in the Prado has a large vase of roses placed directly below her, but as a rule in Northern art the flowers are introduced strictly as symbols to recall some aspect or function of the Virgin or of her Divine Son.

In an ' Adoration ' the surrounding angels bring their roses and their lilies in tribute to the sinless Child.   As Saint Mectilda says:

' The lily figures His innocence and the rose His invincible patience.' [1]

Where the Virgin is seated enthroned, surrounded by saints and angels, even though the Holy Child is upon her knee, all symbols except that which the Child holds in His hand refer again to her.

It is rare, however, that, when holding the Child, she carries her own attribute herself. Usually the symbols, flowers or fruit, are held by angels or laid beside her throne, but in the large ' Enthroned Madonna ' of Signorelli,[2] a painter who showed some originality in his use

[1] *Spiritual Grace.*   [2] Pinacoteca, Arezzo.

of symbols, Mary encircles the Child with her
right arm and in her left hand holds a handsome
stalk of lilies. That the flower refers to the
wonder of her own purity in conjunction with
her motherhood, and not to the Child's sinlessness, is proved by the words on the scroll of the
Prophet Isaiah, who stands below gazing up
at her with rapture:

' Behold a Virgin shall conceive and bear a Son.'

Vasari says of this work:[1] ' In his old age he
painted a picture for the brotherhood of San
Girolamo in Arezzo, partly at the cost of Messer
Niccolò Gamurrini, doctor of laws, and auditor
of the Ruota, whose portrait, taken from life,
is in the picture; he is kneeling before the
Madonna, to whose protection he is recom-
mended by Saint Nicholas. In the same work
are figures of Saint Donatus and Saint Stephen,
with that of Saint Jerome, undraped, beneath;
there is likewise a figure of David singing to a
psaltery with two prophets who are seen, by
the written scrolls which they hold in their

[1] *Lives of the Painters*, Signorelli.

hands, to be engaged in a conference on the conception of the Virgin.'

In another altar-piece by Signorelli[1] it is the Infant Christ who carries the lily, the symbol of His own sinlessness. In this picture all the symbolism refers to the Holy Child, not to the Virgin, which is unusual in an ' Enthroned Madonna.' But the scroll upon the cross of the Baptist, with the words ' *Ecce Agnus Dei,*' directs the devotion of the worshipper to the Son.

In still another of Signorelli's compositions[2] the archangel Michael stands on one side of the Madonna's throne with his scales for the weighing of souls, and Gabriel upon the other side with a large stalk of lilies. The latter carries the lilies, not merely as his own attribute, to denote that he is Gabriel, but also in greeting to the Madonna, for in his other hand he holds a scroll with the words, ' *Ave Maria, gratia plena.*'

There is a Madonna and Child by Fra Angelico,[3] where the Virgin, whose features

---

[1] Cathedral, Perugia.   [2] Accademia, Florence.
[3] Collection Pierpont Morgan, America.

are more strongly marked than is usual with
the Master, holds in her right hand a vase in
which are three roses and a stem of lilies. Her
left arm is round the Child, whose little hand
grasps a single lily cup. The composition is
not pleasing, for the Mother is embarrassed
and encumbered by the great vase; also the
symbolism is not very clear, but apparently
the roses and the lily in the vase are the attributes of Mary, while the flower in His hand refers
to the Holy Child.

There are very few flowers which are
placed within the hand of the Madonna.
In Italy she sometimes holds the *lilium
candidum* of the virgin saints in her character of Queen of Virgins. In Germany and
the Tyrol the large white lily is replaced
by the native lily-of-the-valley; and in the
' Madonna with the Siskin ' ¹ of Albert Dürer
she accepts some sprays of the sweet-
scented white bells from the hand of the
tiny Saint John. In many pictures she
holds a rose. Apart from symbolism, a
flower was a fitting thing to grace a woman's

¹ Kaiser Friedrich Museum, Berlin.

hand, and the rose was considered the fairest
of flowers.

'As the rose is the flower of flowers,
So is Thy House the House of Houses,'

says the ancient inscription within York Minster,
and the rose was *the* flower *par excellence* in every
European country.

But when Mary places the rose within the
hand of the Infant Saviour, then it becomes
His attribute with the full significance of divine
love, and when she places a carnation between
the little fingers, divine love is again expressed.

But, as already noticed, in pictures of
Florentine origin, the rose in the Virgin's hand
has a special meaning, for it illustrates her title
of ' *Madonna del Fiori,*' and the Cathedral of
Florence was dedicated to ' Our Lady of the
Flower.'   Also in pictures painted for some
charitable institution the rose or roses of the
Virgin have still another meaning, for then,
following the interpretation of Raban Maur,
they are the symbol of charity.   One picture
with such roses is that painted by Giambono
for the *Congregazione di Carità* at Fano.   That
these roses are in no way the attribute of the

Child is shown by His attitude, for His back is turned to the hand which holds the flowers.

One of the most beautiful things in the beautiful city of Lucca is the little chapel of Santa Maria della Rosa. It was originally dedicated to Saint Paul and fell into disuse, but in the very earliest years of the fourteenth century a fresco was discovered beneath the creepers which covered the walls. The fresco was even then considered to be extremely ancient, and represented the Virgin with the Child and holding three roses in her hand. In 1309 the Bishop of Lucca conceded to the *Università de' Mercanti* the power to erect on the spot a church dedicated to the Virgin of the Rose and the Apostles Peter and Paul, and the present exquisite little building was commenced.

The outside is ornamented with lovely arabesques of roses in low relief executed in 1333, and upon one angle is a statue of the Virgin with a rose in her hand, possibly by Giovanni Pisano. In the sacristry are the arms of the confraternity figuring Mary surrounded by an oval nimbus and supported by two bushes, which carry thirteen roses, and form a crown

o

from which rise patriarchs and prophets. The original fresco has disappeared.

Very rarely the Virgin holds a violet. The flower is used in Christian art almost exclusively to indicate the humility of the Son of God in taking upon Himself our human form, and in the beautiful altar-piece by Stephen Lochnar [1] the Saviour stretches up His tiny hand to grasp the violet held by Mary, so making it His individual attribute. The panel is rich in colouring, but Mary is of the simple, placid type of the early German school. She is gravely, deeply happy in her motherhood, and not saddened, as in Italy, by painful forebodings. The Child reaches up His hand with a pretty gesture, accepting from her, who had given Him His tender little body, also the violet, symbol of His humility.

In a picture by Bruder Wilhelm [2] the Virgin holds a sweet-pea, bearing both the flower and ripened pods. The symbolism of the pea is obscure and is not to be traced in Christian iconography, though there is the legend of the *erbilia*, a species of pea which, springing first from the footsteps of Saint Columban, still

[1] Cologne.   [2] Cologne.

grows upon the Tuscan mountains. Possibly the symbolism may lie in the simultaneous flowering and fruiting of the pea, for the palm was held by some writers to be an emblem of the Virgin, and for the reason that 'it flowered and fruited at one and the same time.' [1]

There are three subjects, all connected with the Virgin's death, where lilies are once more found. They are her Ascension, the Giving of her Girdle to Saint Thomas, and her Coronation. In each of these the flower-filled tomb, from which she has just arisen, is introduced, usually as the base of the composition.

But the lilies in these pictures do not refer to the immaculate purity of the Virgin Mother, but represent the souls of ' angels, confessors and virgins.' The legends which the *Legenda Aurea* contains were collected by Jacobus de Voragine during the last half of the thirteenth century, while the lily was still the flower of virgin martyrs and was not yet the Madonna's lily. He gives the following account of the burial of the Virgin:

' The Lord commanded the Apostles that they should carry the body into the valley of

[1] W. Menzel, *Christliche Symbolik.*

Jehoshaphat and place it in a new tomb that had been dug there, and watch three days beside it, till He should return.

'And straightway there surrounded her flowers of roses, which are the blessèd company of martyrs; and lilies of the valley, which are the bands of angels, confessors and virgins.'

But the *Byzantine Guide to Painting*, in the paragraph entitled ' How to represent the Assumption of the Divine Mother,' directs that in the lower part of the picture there should be ' an open and empty tomb.'

There was therefore divergence of opinion, and the Church apparently left the artist free.

Jacobus de Voragine seems to have collected the many floating legends of the Virgin, and with that poetic judgment which was the peculiar gift of his generation, to have preserved those forms particularly marked by sweetness or distinction of incident.   But some even of his own countrymen apparently preferred the legend in its balder form, for the astonished Apostles surround a bare and empty tomb. Beyond the Alps, where the *Legenda Aurea* never had much influence, the tomb is almost invariably empty, and indeed all three subjects are rare in the North, though the death of the Virgin is frequently represented.

The majority of Italian painters, however, gladly seized the pretty detail, and the Virgin's tomb is usually flower-filled. But the painters of the high Renaissance did not keep strictly to the symbolism of the legend. There is a beautiful fresco by Sodoma,[1] in which the Virgin, dignified and lovely, ascends from a tomb brimming over with roses, and from among them springs one mystic lily.

Raphael,[2] too, gives a single lily rising from among the roses, and both he and Sodoma seem to have adopted the later fashion of considering the lily as exclusively the Virgin Mary's flower, and instead of serried lilies, representing bands of angels and virgin saints, they paint one only flower, emblem of the Queen of Virgins rising to Heaven attended by the glowing souls of martyrs.

Botticelli,[3] on the other hand, has left the roses and painted lilies only, lilies crowded to-

[1] Oratory of S. Bernardino, Siena.   [2] Vatican.
[3] National Gallery (now attributed to Botticini).

gether in such a mass of loveliness that the mourners seem blinded even to the gorgeous bow of angels in the sky and to the greater wonder in the opening heavens high above.

Benozzo Gozzoli [1] gives the flower-filled tomb, but neglects the symbolism of the legend, for to the roses he adds daisies and jasmine. It is simply a collection of the flowers sacred to the Virgin.

Giulio Romano,[2] in the *Madonna di Monteluce*, paints neither roses nor lilies, merely small, indeterminate blossoms, mauve, blue and yellow.

On one panel,[3] of the fifteenth century, which represents ' The Giving of the Girdle to Saint Thomas,' cut roses and lilies lie upon the top of the closed tomb, which seems a misapprehension of the legend, but possibly the artist merely intended to paint the flowers usually used as attributes of the Virgin—the rose of love and the lily of purity—without any reference to the story as told in the Golden Legend.

But though the lilies of the Virgin's tomb represent angels and virgin saints, in those pictures of her Coronation or Assumption, where

[1] Vatican.   [2] Vatican.   [3] Cathedral, Bagno di Romagna.

no tomb is shown, the flower is the symbol of her own purity. Through her perfect purity she has attained the crown, therefore it is with stems of white lilies that the rose-crowned angels hail her Queen.

Fra Filippo Lippi [1] paints her kneeling to receive the crown from God the Father:

> ' Ringed by a bowery, flowery angel-brood
> Lilies and vestments and white faces, sweet
> As puff on puff of grated orris-root.' [2]

A child-angel holds a scroll with the words:

> ' *Is perfecit opus*,'

and the archangel Gabriel with a lily, painted in a small lunette above the throne, recalls the first beginning of the work now perfected; while before the throne, and thick on either side, is a waving grove of large white lilies, each stalk held by an adoring angel.

The devotional figure of the Virgin known as the ' Immaculate Conception ' is usually presented as the woman with ' the moon under her feet, and upon her head a crown of twelve stars;' four or five attendant child-angels each

---

[1] Accademia, Florence.   [2] Robert Browning.

carry a symbol of her virtues, and the lily is always prominent among them.

This particular aspect of the Virgin was especially popular in Spain, where Murillo was its finest exponent. The flowers of an Immaculate Conception are the rose, lily, olive and palm, signifying love, purity, peace and victory. Sometimes the iris, the royal lily, is added; sometimes it replaces the *lilium candidum*. José Antolines [1] paints the iris only.

In the chapter on 'Garlands of Roses' we remarked the thorns which in the mystic Enclosed Gardens of Germany illustrate the verse:

'As a lily among thorns, so is my love among the daughters.'

With the closing of the fifteenth century these thorn trellises passed from Northern art, but the application of the metaphor to the Virgin still persisted in Northern theology, and since the Immaculate Conception had replaced the *Hortus Conclusus* as a devotional subject, it is as an attribute of the Virgin, risen to glory, that we find the thorns, and in an Immaculate Conception by Seghers [2] a child-angel flutters

[1] Alte Pinakothek, Munich.   [2] Uffizi, Florence.

at the Madonna's feet with a lily enclosed in branches of thorns.

In the 24th chapter of Ecclesiasticus there is a description of Wisdom with her attributes in which the Roman Catholic Church has seen a prefiguring of the Virgin Mary. Some pictorial renderings of the Immaculate Conception make special reference to this, notably the large altar-piece, of unknown authorship, but believed to date from the end of the fifteenth century, which was painted for the Church of S. Francesco in Lucca.[1]

In the upper part of the picture Christ is seen seated, and holding out above the kneeling Virgin the sceptre of His royal favour. Above the sceptre is a scroll with the words from the Book of Esther: ' Not for thee was this law made, but for all mankind.' She alone was immaculate. Around there is a wreath of angels. Below stand King David, King Solomon, Saint Augustine, Saint Anselm and Saint Anthony of Padua. Behind these figures stretches a charming garden. Against the horizon are the cypresses of Mount Zion, the cedar of Lebanon,

[1] Now in the Pinacoteca, Lucca.

the palm tree of Cades, and also a pomegranate
laden with fruit. Midway there is a rose hedge
thick with the roses of Jericho. A terrace runs
across the garden, and upon the parapet are two
stone vases, one labelled *Mirra* and the other
Balsamum.

These trees and plants are the trees and plants
to which Wisdom, and therefore Mary, is likened
in Ecclesiasticus, with the pomegranate of the
Canticles.

'Quasi cedrus exaltata sum in Libano, et
quasi cypressus in Monte Sion: quasi palma
exaltata sum in Cades, et quasi plantatio rosae
in Jericho: . . . Sicut cinnamomum et balsamum aromatizans odorem dedi: quasi myrrha
electa dedi suavitatem odoris.[1]

'Emissiones tuae paradisus malorum puni-
corum cum pomorum fructibus.'[2]

[1] Ecclesiasticus xxiv. 17, 18, 20.
[2] *Cant. Cantic.* iv. 13.

XVIII

THE LILY OF THE SAINTS

THE ancient Hebrews took the lily as the symbol of chastity. The name of the chaste woman of the apocryphal story was Susannah, in Hebrew Shusan, which signifies a lily. The derivation was not forgotten by German artists, for a lily is usually conspicuous in the elaborate garden scenes in which they set this subject, though the Italians reserved the flower for the Madonna and the saints of the monastic orders.

Originally the lily was given to all virgin saints, and it was considered their special attribute before the flower was particularly associated with the Virgin Mary.

> ' Jesus, corona virginum
> Qui pergis inter lilia
> Septis choreis virginum
> Sponsus decorus gloria.'

In the Catacombs there are no virgin martyrs depicted, and the few lilies found there represent merely the flora of Heaven with the general significance of celestial bliss. In the early mosaics, too, both in Ravenna and Rome, the lilies are decorative and the virgins carry crowns of victory.

But as early as the ninth century the lily is used pictorially as the indication of virginity in the famous Beneditional of Saint Ethelwold of Winchester.[1] The Saxon queen, Saint Ethelreda (Saint Audry), who leads the choir of virgin saints, wears the Benedictine habit, is crowned, and holds in one hand the gospel and in the other a lily. She founded Ely Cathedral and, at least after her second marriage, lived as a nun. The miniature was executed in 980.

In the Church of S. Chiara in Naples there is a picture executed in mosaic of the early Christian martyr, Saint Reparata. The mosaic, which is of the thirteenth century, is attributed to Cavallini, and the saint has a lily by her side.

But after the thirteenth century the lily is given almost exclusively to saints of the monastic orders, the higher distinction of the palm being awarded to the martyrs. ' For,' says Durandus, ' the Martyrdom taketh precedence of the

---

[1] In Collection of the Duke of Devonshire.

Virginity; because it is a sign of the more perfect love: according as the Truth saith, " Greater
love hath no man than this, that a man lay down
his life for his friends.' "

Occasionally these early saints are given the
lily in addition to the palm. Mantegna paints
Saint Euphemia with a lily in the right hand
and a palm in the left.[1] But usually they have
the palm alone. The lilies of Saint Cecilia
allude to the celestial lilies of her legend.

À propos of Saint Cecilia, Chaucer's very
charming, if fanciful, derivation of her name
may be recalled:

> ' First wol I you the name of Sainte Cecilie
> Expoune as men may in hire storie see:
> It is to sayn in English, Hevens lilie,
> For pure chasteness of virginitee,
> Or for she whitnesse had of honestee,
> And grene of conscience, and of good fame
> The swote savour, lilie was her name.'

Since the lily was appropriated by the celi-
bates of the Church another symbol had to be
found for the chastity of those still in the world,
and for the virtue of the secular the unicorn was
chosen. The mediæval legend ran that the

[1] Cremona.

unicorn was of all created beasts the fiercest and most difficult to capture. But should a maid be in his path he would lie down with his head upon her lap and then the hunter could take him with great ease.

'The Triumph of Chastity' with the 'Triumph of Love' as a pendant were rather favourite subjects in the fifteenth century in Italy, particularly as a decoration of the elaborate bridal chests or *cassoni*, then in vogue. 'The Triumph of Chastity' of Liberale da Verona [1] is typical. The white-clothed figure of a young woman stands upon a car drawn by unicorns, while behind follows a rejoicing crowd. She holds a cornucopia but no lily appears.

On the shutters in the Hall of Heliodorus, in the Vatican, there is a very beautiful Renaissance design in which the lily and the unicorn are united, but usually in Italy the lily was kept as an ecclesiastical and the unicorn as a secular symbol.

In German art both lily and unicorn are held to be symbols of the Virgin's purity, and in the fourteenth and fifteenth centuries there

[1] Museum, Verona.

were many tapestries and embroideries executed in the convents illustrating that strange allegorical version of the Annunciation known as ' The Hunting of the Unicorn.' But the unicorn is never associated with the monastic saints, and indeed, in Northern art, monastic saints themselves are rather rare.

The lily was, therefore, latterly the symbol of monastic celibacy. There is a curious allegorical picture of Saint Francis by Sassetta. The present owner, Mr B. Behrenson, describes it thus:

' Over the sea and the land, into the golden heavens, towers the figure of the blessed Francis, his face transfigured with ecstasy, his arms held out in his favourite attitude of the cross, his feet firmly planted on a prostrate warrior in golden panoply. Cherubim and Seraphim, with fiery wings and deep crescent halos, form behind the saint a nimbus framing a glory of gold and azure, as dazzling as the sky and as radiant as the sun. Overhead, on opalescent cloudlets, float Poverty in her patched dress, looking up with grateful devotion, Obedience in her rose-red robe with a yoke about her neck and her hands crossed on her breast, and Chastity in white, holding a lily.' [1]

All three maidens are attractive, and Chastity the prettiest of the three, unlike the immured ' Castitas ' of Giotto,[2] whose guards, with surely unnecessary vigour, drive off ' Amor ' with pitch-forks.

The two men not in holy orders, who are permitted to carry the lily, are Saint John the Baptist and Saint Joseph. The former, even if he took no formal vow of celibacy, is looked upon as the first of the Christian anchorites, and the lily of Saint Joseph is the symbol of the self-abnegation of his married life.

The history of the marriage of the Virgin Mary is found in the apocryphal ' Gospel of the Birth of Mary,' translated by Saint Jerome and abridged in the *Catalogus Sanctorum* of Peter de Natalibus.

' And when Mary was fourteen years of age the High Priest commanded that the virgins brought up in the temple should return home and be wedded according to law. And all

---

[1] A Sienese painter of the Franciscan Legend.
[2] Upper Church, Assisi.

obeyed except Mary, who replied that she might not, as her parents had dedicated her to the Lord and she herself had vowed her virginity to God. And the High Priest, being perplexed by Mary's vow (which ought to be kept) on the one hand, and the introduction of a new custom in Israel on the other, summoned the elders together to consult upon the matter. And as they prayed, a voice came from the sanctuary commanding that every man of the house of David, who was not wedded, should place his rod on the altar, and he whose rod should bud, and the Holy Spirit descend upon it in the form of a dove, according to the prophecy of Isaiah, should be the spouse of Mary.

' And there was among the rest a certain Joseph of the House of David, an old man and a widower, and who had sons and grandsons. And thinking it unseemly that an aged man should marry a tender virgin, when the others presented their rods he withheld his own. And no miracle appearing, the High Priest inquired of the Lord, who answered that he only to whom the Virgin was to be espoused had not presented his rod. So Joseph was brought forward, and

P

presented his rod, and straightway it budded, and the dove descended from heaven and settled upon it. And it was clear to all men that Mary was to be his wife.'

In one of the earliest representations[1] which we have of the ' Marriage of the Virgin ' Joseph holds a stalk of *lilium candidum* with a single flower at its summit, on which is poised the holy dove. Thus Giotto, always thoughtful and original in his symbolism, modified the legendary flowering staff to the flower which should symbolize Saint Joseph's wedded life with the Virgin.

But the great majority of artists have followed the legend more closely. Taddeo Gaddi[2] gives a bunch of leaves at the staff's top, just such leaves as would sprout from a staff of ash. There is only one tiny bud upon the bare stick above which the dove hovers in the ' Marriage ' attributed to Firoenzo di Lorenzo,[3] and Gaudenzio Ferrari[4] paints a scarcely-budded staff.

Sometimes in the sixteenth and seventeenth centuries the staff of Saint Joseph bears red or

[1] Capella dell' Arena, Padua.
[2] Capella Baroncelli, Santa Croce, Florence.
[3] S. Girolamo Spello.   [4] Cathedral, Como.

pink flowers resembling the oleander, and to-day the country people in Tuscany call the oleander *Il Mazzo di San Giuseppe*, that is, ' The Staff of Saint Joseph.'

Northern art, uninfluenced by the *Legenda Aurea*, gives Saint Joseph no flowering staff. Lucas van Leyden[1] paints him as an entirely unidealized workman with tools upon his back but places the lily in his hand. And he has also a lily in the ' Holy Family' of Geertgen tot Sint Jans,[2] though in the many representations of ' The Adoration of the Magi' in North Germany and the Netherlands he is undistinguished by any attribute.

After the seventeenth century Saint Joseph began to have a status of his own as patron of married virtue. Single figures of him appear carrying a lily, not a staff, and in the ecclesiastical art of the present day he carries sometimes the Child-Christ and sometimes a book, but also invariably a lily. A large oleograph which hangs in the Church of the Angels at La Verna shows the Child-Christ crowning him with a wreath of lilies.

Occasionally the lily is given to young girls

[1] Alte Pinakothek, Munich.   [2] Rijks Museum, Amsterdam.

who are neither saints nor martyrs. There is an engraving from a gold medal in the royal library at Windsor of the Empress Leonora of Portugal. The portrait is half-length, standing, with long hair, beneath the arched imperial crown, and she holds in her hand a lily stem with two flowers and three buds. It is inscribed:

‘ Leonora Augusta Frederici Imp. Uxor.’

She was the daughter of King Edward of Portugal and wife of Frederick of Austria, also great-grand-daughter of John of Gaunt. It is a pretty figure, childish but dignified. The long hair, Mr Augustus Franks points out,[1] is generally looked upon as the mark of a virgin bride, and it is explained by her coronation having taken place before the consummation of the marriage. The lily also, like the flowing hair, proclaims her maidenhood.

But, as a rule, the *lilium candidum* is strictly a flower of the church. Paul Veronese[2] painted a Juno with a white lily, but the flower has sharply turned-back petals resembling the turn-cap variety and gracefully curving stems.

[1] *Archæologia*, vol. 45.   [2] Villa Masèr, near Treviso.

It was not till the eighteenth century that Cipriani and Bartolozzi, both members of the English Royal Academy, could design and engrave a heathen goddess, who, with one hand caressing a peacock, held in the other the traditional symbol of virginal innocence.

Lilies are proper to all virgin saints.

> 'Liliis Sponsus recubat, rosisque;
> Tu, tuo semper bene fida Sponso
> Et rosas Martyr simil et dedisti
> Lilia Virgo.'

But some carry them as a special distinction.

Among them Saint Catharine of Siena comes first. She was still merely one of the many children of a working tanner of Siena, her sanctity unrecognized, when she was sent a dream from Heaven. In her dream she saw Saint Dominic, who held in one hand a lily which, like the burning bush of Moses, burned but was not consumed. With his other hand he offered her the black and white habit of the Dominican Tertiaries. Saint Catharine regarded the dream as a definite call and later joined the third Order of Saint Dominic. She was a woman not only of most saintly life but of wonderful force of character, and intervened with altruistic motives and plain common sense in the complicated politics of her day. She experienced the mystical trances which were the crown of holiness to the mediæval mind, and was remarkable also for the austerities and good works which her devoted friend and biographer, Raimondo da Capua, likens to lilies.

'Taught, nay rather compelled, by her supreme Teacher, she learned every day more and more both to enjoy the embraces of the Celestial Bridegroom in the bed of flowers, and to descend into the valley of lilies to make herself more fruitful, nor ever to leave or lessen the one for the sake of the other.'

The most interesting of the pictures of Saint Catharine is that by her friend and disciple, Andrea Vanni,[1] and which is therefore a portrait from memory, if not from life. It was probably painted at the time of her canonization, thirteen years after her death, and shows her as a tall, slight woman with a refined enthusiastic face. In her left hand she holds the lilies[2] which re-

[1] S. Domenico, Siena.
[2] The name Catharine, it will be remembered, is from the Greek *Katharos*, which has the same signification as the lily, *i.e.*, purity.

present the austere virtues of a monastic life. She is the most distinguished woman who wore the veil, and since she is almost invariably represented with a lily, the *lilium candidum* is sometimes called Saint Catharine's lily.

Saint Scholastica of the Benedictines [1] and Saint Clare of the Franciscans are also usually depicted with lilies. The last, who styled herself the Little Flower of Saint Francis, has met with great good fortune at the hands of the painters, for two at least, Simone Martini [2] and Luca Signorelli, [3] have very beautifully materialized her sweetness and humility.

Pictures which represent the mystic espousals of any nun usually have the lily as a detail.

Chief among the monks who carry the flower is Saint Dominic. He was a Spaniard and had all the chivalrous Spanish devotion to the person of the Virgin. It was he who arranged the rosary and instituted it as a religious exercise. He founded a community of preachers for the conversion of heretics, which afterwards

[1] Luini, S. Maurizio, Milan.   [2] S. Francesco, Assisi.
[3] Royal Gallery, Berlin.

developed into the great Dominican order. The great aim of his life was to guard the purity of the Catholic faith, and to this end he hunted forth the Albigenses with his hounds of the Lord —the *Domini canes*. He is rewarded with the lily which, in his picture by Bellini,[1] has a singularly rigid stem.

During the thirteenth, fourteenth and fifteenth centuries sainted monks were comparatively rarely painted, preference being given to the more picturesque figures of the early martyrs who suffered under Roman persecutions. But the earliest to appear, and the most frequently seen, is Saint Dominic. Duccio di Buoninsegna puts him beside the Madonna; Orcagna painted him among the happy souls in the Paradise of Santa Maria Novella. And the reason why he, rather than the other great founders, should appear in heavenly groups is not the fine relief of his black habit among the gay gowns of the angels, but because his order spent their gold on painted decorations at a time when the Franciscans, vowed to poverty, and the Benedictines, devoted to the making

[1] National Gallery, London.

and collecting of books, had less to spend on the encouragement of art. Later, in the sixteenth and seventeenth centuries, and more particularly in Spain, saints in all habits constantly appear.

Saint Dominic almost always carries a lily. Saint Francis was sufficiently distinguished by the stigmata, Saint Benedict by the chalice; but Saint Dominic has a lily white as the austerity of his faith.

Saint Anthony of Padua is to-day the most popular of all the monastic saints. His sane and gentle piety and his reputation for granting little ordinary boons has endeared him to simple folk. There seems no particular reason why he, above other saintly monks, should be so distinguished, but when he is not represented with the Infant Christ in his arms he invariably has a lily. In the very beautiful ' Vision of Saint Anthony,' by Murillo,[1] where the Holy Child appears in a ray of light, a vase of lilies stands upon the table. In another picture, by Annibale Caracci, the Child-Christ Himself holds the lily.

[1] Seville Cathedral.

Another bearer of the lily is he

> ' Whom Mary's charms
> Embellish'd, as the sun the morning star '—

Saint Bernard of Clairvaux.

Though opposing the doctrine of the Immaculate Conception of the Virgin, he had a very special devotion to the Mother of Christ.

Many of his sermons, called by Henault *Chefs d'œuvre de sentiment et de force,* celebrate her perfections, and, in particular, the famous series of sermons upon the Bride of the Song of Solomon.

It is said that it was his love for the ' lily of the valleys ' which so impressed the lily form upon the architecture of his order, for again and again in the Gothic stone-work of the Cistercian abbeys ' lily work ' is found.

The lily, it may be remarked, is given to those saints in holy orders who were pious from their earliest youth and not to those who had passed a gay time in the world before conversion.

XIX

THE VINE

THE principal of the allegorical fruits is the vine. It is one of the most ancient emblems of Christ, and is founded upon His own words, ' I am the vine, ye are the branches.'

It is seen in the Catacombs, on early Christian sarcophagi, and in the early mosaics, always as the emblem of Christ or of His Church. A fruiting vine very beautifully expresses a perfect life rich with the fruits of the spirit, and even were the analogy not suggested by Christ's own words, it is possible that Christians would have seen in the tree whence comes the sacramental wine, emblem of the holy blood, a likeness to Him who shed that blood.

Where the cross, the sacred monogram or the figure of Christ Himself is introduced, the vine takes a secondary place as emblem of the Christian Church, and taken in this sense the symbolism admits of some complication, twelve bunches of grapes typifying the twelve Apostles, and birds among the branches Christian souls.

One example among many of its decorative and symbolical use is on the gravestone of Saint Cummian, an Irish bishop, who died a monk at Bobbio about the middle of the eighth century. Two vine branches spring from the holy chalice and form a border of oval arabesques, one oval enclosing fruit and leaves, the next framing a star alternately. At the top, where the two branches almost meet, are two doves standing on either side of the holy monogram.

The vine is the Christian Church, springing from the chalice of Christ's blood; the fruit represents the good works of the righteous; the stars which shine through the branches Christian hope. The doves, by the convention of the Catacombs, signify departed Christian souls adoring Christ, who is represented by the ancient star monogram, formed of the two Greek letters, $I = Iota$, and $X = Chi$, enclosed in the circle which is the symbol of eternity. The gravestone was executed by order of King Luitprand, and, by an oversight not unique among Christian marbles before the twelfth century, the border has been placed reversed round the inscription—the doves, with their feet in the air, being at the bottom.

As directly emblematical of Christ Himself the vine received the place of honour in all Christian churches, and, even when our Lord was represented in His own person, it was often there by right of its secondary significance as the Church of God—' Ye are the branches.' A mosaic in the Church of Saint Prisca[1] shows a half-length figure of Christ framed in branches of vine, and the golden branches, often intricately wreathed against a dark-blue ground, occur repeatedly in the early mosaics.

But when it grew more usual not only to represent Christ in His own person but also the martyrs, saints and prophets of the Church, the use of the vine became decorative rather than devotional, and was chiefly applied to the ornamentation of vestments, altar-cloths and the vessels used in the celebration of the Eucharist. When, in a painting, the vine is introduced as the emblem of Christ or His Church, it is usually in some detail, as in the very

[1] Rome.

beautiful design of the Pelican in its Piety among grapes and vine leaves behind the figure of God the Father, King of Heaven, in Hubert van Eyck's magnificent altar, ' The Adoration of the Lamb.' [1]

Botticelli, who handled symbols with a depth of sentiment unknown to art before, paints grapes with a different significance. For him grapes, like the Eucharistic wine, are the symbol of the Holy Blood, and in one of the most beautiful and unaffected of all his pictures [2] an angel, standing beside the Infant Christ, holds grapes and corn ears, symbols of the sacrifice of His death.

The Northern symbolists, also, took clustering grapes to have the same value as the Eucharistic wine as an emblem of Christ's blood. This is clearly seen in a tapestry of the fourteenth century, formerly in the Spitzer Collection. The Infant Christ, seated between the Virgin and Saint Joseph, presses with His hands the juice of a bunch of purple grapes into a chalice.

Another Flemish tapestry of the same period, which was also in the same collection, depicts

[1] Ghent Cathedral.   [2] Collection Gardener, Boston.

the Holy Family with Saint Anne. Mary, from whom the Saviour received His human blood, hands to her Son the grapes which He crushes till the wine drops down into the cup.

But the cluster of grapes which several of the Flemish artists place in the hand of the Infant Christ seems to be not only the emblem of the holy blood, but also, in some sort, the antithesis of the apple as the fruit of redemption, which in the hand of the second Adam replaces the fruit of the Fall.

In a picture by Mabuse, inscribed ' Verus Deus et Homo: casta mater et Virgo,' [1] the Virgin offers a bunch of grapes to the Infant Christ, who holds a quince, foreshadowing that He should exchange the fruit of Eden, by which all men died, for the fruit of redemption, by which they shall be saved, and this substitution of the fruit of the vine for the apple of Eden became in the North a rather favourite variation of the symbolism of the fruit of the Tree of Knowledge of Good and Evil.

[1] Berlin.

XX

THE FRUIT OF THE TREE OF KNOWLEDGE

THE Scriptures give no indication whatever as to the size, shape or colour of the Fruit of the Tree of Knowledge of Good and Evil which grew in the midst of Eden, and it has been variously interpreted. Adam is depicted with an apple, a pear, a quince, a fig, according to the individual opinion of the painter. Milton took the tree to be an apple:

> ' A goodly tree . . . .
> Laden with fruit of fairest colours mixt
> Ruddie and gold . . .
> Sharp desire I had
> Of tasting those fair apples.' [1]

And the majority of artists have chosen that fruit. It grew in every part of Europe, and, except the cherry, it was almost the only cultivated fruit in Germany and the Netherlands.

[1] *Paradise Lost.*

Besides grapes, figs and pomegranates it is the only fruit mentioned in Scripture, and it is also possible that some found reason for identifying it with the fruit which brought sin into the world in the apparent similarity of the two Latin words, ' mălum '=evil, and ' mālum '= an apple.

And as the fruit varies in the hand of Adam so it varies in the hand of the Infant Christ, the second Adam. Memling and the painters of Cologne depict Him with an apple. Il Moretto paints a pear,[1] Giovanni Bellini a quince,[2] and Botticelli a pomegranate.[3] The Eve of Jan van Eyck holds a lemon,[4] but he keeps to the older convention in the symbols which he places in the hand of the Infant Saviour: the bird, emblem of the human soul, the inscribed scroll or the cross-surmounted orb.

The apple, when in the hand of Adam, is always the symbol of the Fall; when in the hand of Christ, it is the symbol of the sin of the world which He took upon Himself. ' For as in Adam

---

[1] Vatican.
[2] Uffizi.
[3] Brera, Milan.
[4] Museum, Brussels.

Q

all die, even so in Christ shall all be made alive.'

But in the early instances of a fruit in the Christ-Child's hand it does not appear to be definitely the death-giving apple of Eden. It is fruit of Paradise, a delight promised to the blessed which the King of Heaven brings down with Him to earth.

In the early school of Siena, as we have already seen, the little Christ was still the Royal Infant, still ' trailing clouds of glory,' untouched by shadow of suffering, and usually bearing in His hand some indication of His high estate. Often His hand was raised in blessing, sometimes He held a lily of Paradise.

On an early fourteenth-century panel in the manner of the Lorenzetti, in Siena Academy, the Child holds a fruit, but it is not clearly defined. In one of Sano di Pietro's most attractive works,[1] however, which is dated 1444, the Child, seated on the Virgin's knee, holds a golden orange with its foliage. To His right and left are saints, and close around there are six angels crowned with blue corn-flowers and carrying roses

[1] Belle Arti, Siena.

and lilies. No attempt is made to realize earthly conditions; the glowing scene is set in Heaven, and the little Lord of Heaven holds in His hand a celestial fruit, just one of such fruits as hang upon the trees in Giovanni di Paolo's ' Paradise.' [1]

In another picture by Sano di Pietro,[2] the Child (perhaps the most charming ' Bambino ' ever painted in Siena) holds in His hand a bunch of cherries.

Cherries, painted more than once within the tiny hand by Sano di Pietro, are always taken as the delicious fruit. Like the lilies of the earlier Paradises they typify the delights of the blessed, and in German art particularly they are painted often as the peculiar fruit of Heaven. They are never taken as the Fruit of the Tree of Knowledge of Good and Evil, and therefore, at least in the early Sienese school, this fruit held by the Infant Christ would seem to be the fruit of Paradise.

In Northern art, in the work of the French ivory cutters, and particularly in the work of Memling and of those artists influenced by him, the apple takes precedence of all other symbols

---

[1] Belle Arti, Siena.   [2] *Ibid.*

in the Christ-Child's hand. Northern theologians, studying the Old Testament carefully,
and deeply interested in types and anti-types,
saw in Adam the type of Christ. The *Biblia
Pauperum*, originally designed with the intention of teaching the faith to the unlettered,
served as a pattern-book for stained glass and
other ecclesiastical decoration from the ninth
century onwards. Each page is divided into
three sections. In the centre is a scene from
the life of Christ; in the sections on either side
is a scene from Old Testament History, showing
some incident in the lives of those men who are
considered to be types of Christ, which fore-
shadowed some act of the Redeemer. And
chief of these types is Adam. Therefore in the
Northern Church the idea of Jesus Christ as
the second Adam was familiar, and the fruit in
His hand was perfectly understood as a symbol.
Memling, who, if he did not originate the symbolism of the apple of Eden, made it famous by
constant repetition on his magnificently executed panels, usually treats it quite simply.
The apple is the symbol of the Fall, and therefore of the world's sin, which Christ accepts as

Menling   *Photo Brogi*

THE FRUIT OF HEAVEN RELINQUISHED
FOR THE APPLE OF EDEN

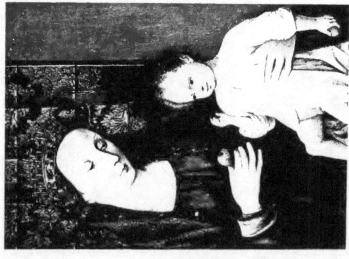

Hugo van der Goes   *Photo Brogi*

THE FRUIT OF DAMNATION EXCHANGED FOR

His own. In the fine example at Chatsworth, the Infant Christ, with one hand pointing to the book of prophecy, takes with the other the apple held by an attendant angel. But one painting by Memling [1] is especially interesting, since it links together the two symbols, the fruit of heavenly bliss and the fruit of Man's redemption. The Child sits upon His mother's knee, and in one hand clutches cherries, the fruit of Paradise. He seems, however, on the point of relinquishing them to take the apple from the angel's hand, as He relinquished heavenly joy to take upon Himself the sin of the world.

Meanwhile the painters of Florence, Fra Angelico, Neri di Bicci, Filippo Lippi and Botticelli, had painted the Child with the pomegranate, and it is not very clear whether they held to the Sienese symbolism or sympathized with the Northern tradition. But it was probably the fruit of Eden, for in all other points the Florentines had broken with the Byzantine conventions, and the Child was for them no longer the Royal Child, richly clothed and dignified in gesture, but He was a little naked

[1] Uffizi.

human baby, born into the world to repair, as the second Adam, the old Adam's fault. That He is the Saviour, rather than the King, is particularly emphasized by Botticelli, who seldom fails, even though it be only by the foreboding in the grey eyes of the angels, to give some hint of the coming tragedy.

On the other hand it may be possible that the painters of Florence in the fifteenth century had harked back to another source for their symbolism and had taken the imagery of Saint Gregory the Great, who used the pomegranate as the emblem of the Christian Church ' because of the inner unity of countless seeds in one and the same fruit.' But in later Italian art, as in all the Northern countries and in modern Church symbolism, the fruit, most usually the apple, which is in the hand of the Infant Christ, is the fruit of redemption, as the apple of Adam was the fruit of damnation.

Following the same analogy, the Virgin is regarded as the second Eve, the second universal mother, who, through her Son, is to repair the fault of the first.

The symbolists of the thirteenth century

found what they considered proof of this in the word of Scripture.

Conrad von Würztburg writes:

> ' Let a man take three letters:
> ' When these straightforward are read,
> The little word " Ave " stands out,
> The new word of salutation (or healing).
> Let him begin at the end,
> And read to the beginning,
> And " Eva " is found written.
>
> .   .   .   .   .
>
> That one may thereby know,
> It is thou who fulfillest,
> The old and the new Covenants.
> The greeting from the angel's mouth
> Greeting thee, O royal spotless maid,
> Hath told me this.' [1]

Therefore the apple, which masters of the Flemish and early German schools sometimes introduced into Annunciations, laying it, for instance, upon the window-sill, is the apple of redemption.

The apple in the hand of Eve is always the apple of damnation. There is a curious drawing by Martin Schöngauer of the ' Descent into Hell.' Adam and Eve come forth first of the

[1] *Goldene Schmiede.*

released souls, Eve holding the apple, which has the marks of her teeth still upon it.

In the hand of Mary it is again the apple of redemption, but it is the fruit of the Fall when it is between the jaws of the serpent or dragon, which she, at her Assumption, treads under foot.

In Italian art the apple is less often found in the Madonna pictures, but the ancient analogy was not forgotten. On the predella of Lorenzo di Credi's ' Annunciation '[1] there are three exquisite little scenes from the life of Eve, and Vasari introduces the Tree of the Knowledge of Good and Evil into his ' Conception of the Virgin,' painted in 1540. Vasari describes it himself:

' The Tree of the Original Sin was represented in the centre of the painting, and at the roots thereof were placed nude figures of Adam and Eve bound, as being the first transgressors of God's commands. To the principal branches there were also bound Abraham, Isaac, Jacob, Moses, Aaron, Joshua, David and the rest of the kings, law-givers, etc., according to their seniority, all fastened by both arms, excepting

[1] Uffizi.

Martin Schöngauer

ADAM AND EVE DELIVERED FROM HELL
(Print Room, Alte Pinakothek, Munich)

To face page 348

only Samuel and Saint John the Baptist, who are bound by one arm only, to intimate that they were sanctified before their birth. At the trunk of the tree, and with the lower part turning around it, is the Old Serpent, but the upper part of the form has the shape of Man, and the hands are confined behind the back; on his head is one foot of the glorious Virgin, which is trampling down the horns of the demon, while the other foot is fixed on a moon. Our Lady is clothed with the sun and crowned with twelve stars, being sustained in the air within a splendour of numerous angels, nude, and illuminated by the rays which proceed from the Madonna herself. These same rays, moreover, passing amidst the foliage of the tree, give light to the figures bound to the branches; nay, they seem to be gradually loosening their bonds, by the power and grace which they derive from her out of whom they proceed. In Heaven, meanwhile, that is, at the highest point of the picture, are two children bearing a scroll, on which are the following words:

' " *Quos Eva culpa damnavit, Mariæ gratia solvit.*" ' [1]

---

[1] *Lives of the Painters.*

It was thus that Vasari united in one picture the two universal mothers, the physical and the spiritual, and his allegory was typical of the mysticism of his day, for he tells us that, being doubtful as to the due treatment of the subject, he and his patron, Messer Bindo, ' took counsel with such of our common friends as were men of letters,' and Vasari's friends included the fine flower of Italian intellect.

The picture, which is a good deal darkened by time, and less interesting than the description leads one to expect, is still in its original place in the Church of SS. Apostoli in Florence.

In some pictures, particularly those showing the influence of Memling, an attendant angel holds the apple, holding it ready till the time shall come when the Infant Saviour, with growing consciousness of His mission, holds forth His hand to take it.

But there are various ' Holy Families ' [1] of the early German school in which Saint Anne

[1] Joos van Cleeve, Royal Gallery, Brussels; Wolf Trant, National Museum, Munich.

sits holding the apple. It seems strange that she should, but it is to be remembered that in German popular religion and in German art Saint Anne holds an important place. Altars were often dedicated to her, and the holy family might, in a manner, be called her attribute. Frequently Saint Anne and the Virgin are depicted seated on one seat, apparently with equal possessive rights over the Holy Child, who stands between them. There is also that strange allegorical conception usually styled ' *Mutter Anna selb-dritt*,' where Saint Anne sits with the Infant Christ on one knee and the Child-Virgin on the other. She was the Virgin's nearest blood-relation, and if the Virgin was without sin, it was Anne, born in sin but the Mother of His Mother, who most nearly connected the incarnate Godhead with the erring human race. It was perhaps fitting, therefore, that she, representing sinful humanity, should offer to the Saviour the fruit of the Fall, which in His hand would become the fruit of Redemption. At other times it is Mary who holds the fruit, but offering it to the Saviour, who raises His hand to take it. She, as the second Eve, places in His hand the apple by which mankind is to be redeemed, not lost, since she, by giving Him a human body, had made that redemption possible.

In the Corsini Gallery[1] there is a picture, attributed to Hugo van der Goes, in which Mother and Child hold each a fruit. At first sight it seems as if it were a presentment in one picture of Christ as the second Adam, and Mary as the second Eve, with a doubling of the symbolism of the apple which would be illogical. But the fruit held by Mary is distinctly a pear, that held by Christ apparently an apple. The artist has, therefore, discriminated between the apple of damnation and the sweeter, mellower fruit, which may be the symbol of Redemption, for the Holy Child seems to be in the act of exchanging one for the other.

This may possibly also explain the thought in the mind of the French ivory-cutters of the fourteenth century, for they, too, not infrequently, placed a small round fruit resembling an apple in the hand of the Infant Christ and a larger pear-shaped fruit in that of His mother,

[1] Florence.

though they give little indication of any action of exchange.

Northern art, though realistic, was very placid, and, except in scenes from the Passion, quite unmarked by the sometimes painful pathos of the Italian and Spanish schools. In the Madonna pictures the only faint reminder of the tragedy for which the Child was born into the world is the rosy-cheeked apple in the tiny hand. The mother is satisfied and untroubled, the Child smiling happily, and an apple is a natural, pleasant thing to place within a baby's hand. Rubens painted a delightful ' Holy Family beneath an Apple Tree ' [1]—a little scene of idyllic happiness; and scarcely noticeable is the pathetic suggestion of the branch of apples which Zacharias holds towards the little Christ.

The shifting of theological and artistic standpoints at the Reformation in no way disturbed the Northern love of Old Testament analogies or the affection for this particular symbol, and in Germany one of its most charming developments was the Christmas tree, the evergreen tree laden with golden and silver apples, set up in every

[1] Imperial Gallery, Vienna.

home to commemorate the birth of Christ. It is the Tree of Eden, which Christ by His birth and death transmuted into a tree of Paradise.

The apple is the most usual fruit in the hand of the Infant Christ, but some Flemish painters of the early sixteenth century give Him grapes instead. The grapes symbolize the divine blood by which souls lost through Adam's fall are redeemed. Gerard David[1] puts a cluster of white grapes in the tiny hand; Lucas van Leyden[2] white grapes also with leaves and tendrils; and in another picture Lucas van Leyden[3] places the apple and the grapes together upon the broad ledge in the foreground. In this last there is the same idea of exchange which is found more clearly expressed in the picture by Mabuse at Berlin.

This substitution of the fruit of the vine for the apple of Eden seems only to be found in the Netherlands. In a very beautiful picture by Botticelli, the grapes held by the angel have a simpler meaning. They, with the corn, are the direct emblems of the body and the blood of the Saviour, and foretell the coming sacrifice

[1] Museum, Rouen.   [2] Alte Pinakothek, Munich.
[3] Kaiser Friedrich Museum, Berlin.

of His death; the symbolism is identical with
that of the embroidered vine-leaves and wheat-
ears of so many modern altar frontals.[1]

Very often, as upon the façade of Orvieto
Cathedral, the fig-tree is taken as the Tree of
Temptation, for, it might be argued, our first
parents would take to make themselves garments
the leaves of the tree nearest to their hand, the
leaves of that same tree of whose fruit they had
just eaten. ' It is possible that the erotic significance which the fig had among the ancients
was also considered in this connection,'[2] and it
is probably because of its classical associations
that the fig was never placed in the hand of the
Infant Saviour.

Except as the forbidden fruit the fig is not
found in Italian or Flemish ecclesiastical art,
but in Germany there appears to have been no
prejudice against it. It is painted frequently
in the Madonna pictures. A small fig-tree over-
shadows the cot of the Infant Christ in a picture
by Matthias Grünewald;[3] Hans Burgkmair[4]

[1] The ' Chigi ' Madonna, Collection Gardener, Boston.
[2] W. Menzel, *Christliche Symbolik.*   [3] Museum. Colmar.
[4] German Museum, Nüremburg.

paints it with the rose, the iris, the columbine and other attributes of the Virgin; Hans Holbein [1] the Younger sets his Saint Ursula against a fig-tree; and it is the only growing thing introduced in his best-known work, the beautiful Madonna of the Bürgomeister Meyer.[2]

These fig-trees, unlike the barren fig-tree of Scripture, always bear fruit and appear to be the symbols of a holy life rich with the fruits of the Spirit.

[1] Kunsthalle, Karlsruhe.   [2] Royal Gallery, Dresden.

XXI

THE GOURD

In the works of Crivelli, who painted in the cities of the Marches between 1468 and 1493, the apple repeatedly occurs with a gourd laid close beside it. In the ' Annunciation ' [1] they are together upon the foreground's edge. In ' The Infant Christ giving the Keys to Saint Peter ' [2] the apple lies on the ground and the gourd is suspended on the right hand of the throne. In the triptych in the Brera they hang forward prominently from the wreath above the Madonna's head. They are again suspended, singly, each side of the head of Saint Giacomo della Marca [3] (sometimes taken to be Saint Bernadine), toning with the colour scheme, which has all the subdued richness of old Cordova leather; and exactly the same apple and gourd lie on a ledge before the ' Madonna with the Child ' by Francia, [4] and

[1] National Gallery. [2] Museum, Berlin.
[3] Vatican Gallery. [4] Capitoline Museum, Rome.

have the identical position in an ' Enthroned Madonna ' by Lorenzo da San Severino.[1]

As the grouping of these two fruits is so insistently repeated there is reason to think that it was no chance arrangement. The painter seems to attach some definite meaning to their juxtaposition, and since not Crivelli only, but also Francia and Lorenzo da San Severino, place them together, and well forward in the picture where the eye cannot miss them, they are apparently recognized symbols, not the whim of a single painter.

The apple is, probably, here as elsewhere, the fatal fruit of Eden, and the gourd may represent the fruit which is to be the antidote, in the same sense that the grape is occasionally used by painters of the early Flemish school. In this case the gourd would represent the Resurrection and be the revival of a very ancient symbol which has an interesting history. Among the wall paintings of the Catacombs the story of Jonah is very repeatedly found. He is taken as the type of the risen Christ,[2] since Christ

[1] National Gallery.
[2] " For as Jonas was three days and three nights in the whale's belly; so shall the Son of Man be three days and three nights in the heart of the earth " (Matt. xii. 40).

Himself, answering the Pharisees, made the comparison. He is represented both as being cast up by the fish and, in the ensuing incident of his history, reposing under the gourd on the east side of the city of Nineveh. The first subject being certainly grotesque, it became more usual to depict him beneath the booth covered with long-shaped gourds, and his sleeping figure (usually with the legs crossed) is found constantly both among the Catacomb paintings and on fragments of the early Christian gilded glass. Above him there is always the same pergola-like booth with the hanging gourds. One small disk of gold-ornamented Catacomb glass [1] has upon it the usual gourd, but below, in place of Jonah, there is a large fish (Ichthys), an emblem of Christ dating from the second century. Thus the type of Christ has been replaced by His emblem, but the gourd, by association symbol of His Resurrection, remains.

Therefore in these pictures by Crivelli the apple would be the symbol of our death by the act of Adam, and the gourd of our Resurrection by the act of the second Adam, Jesus Christ.

[1] Vatican Museum.

In a picture of the Fall, painted in 1570 by Floris Francesco of Antwerp,[1] Adam sits upon the ground while Eve offers him an apple from the tree. On the earth beside Adam lies a very large gourd. This gourd may only exemplify the fruitfulness of Eden, or it may be another example of the antithetical use of this symbol.

[1] Uffizi, Florence.

XXII

THE POMEGRANATE

NERI DI BICCI,[1] Fra Angelico,[2] Filippo Lippi [3] and other artists of the fifteenth century painted the Infant Saviour with a pomegranate in His hand.

On the wall of the Bargello,[4] in the Chapel of the Podestà, is a frescoed Paradise, which contains a figure long believed to be a portrait of Dante by Giotto. He is seen in profile, wearing the characteristic hood, and holds in his hand a small branch on which are two ripe pomegranates. The fresco is not now considered to be by Giotto, nor the portrait contemporaneous, but that would not materially affect the meaning of the pomegranates, if they be a symbol, since the painting dates from the last half of the fourteenth century.

Were it not for Dante's pomegranate there

[1] Uffizi.
[2] Accademia, Florence.
[3] Pitti.
[4] Florence.

would be no particular reason to think that the artists of the ' Quattrocento ' meant more than simply to indicate some heavenly fruit when they placed the pomegranate in the hand of the Child Christ. In accordance with the Byzantine tradition to which Siena held, they regarded Him as the Royal Child come to earth with Heavenly gifts in His hand; they had not yet adopted the symbolism of the North, which saw in the Infant Christ the second Adam, holding the fruit of the Tree of Knowledge of Good and Evil, though indeed Botticelli, who almost always gives some indication of coming sorrow in Christ's childhood, seems to have found some sad inner meaning in the symbol.

But in Dante's hand the fruit could not be the fruit of Paradise, and it may therefore have some further meaning even when held by the Infant Saviour.

Walter Pater writes: ' The mystical fruit, which because of the multitude of its seeds was to the Romans a symbol of fecundity . . . to the middle age became a symbol of the fruitful earth itself; and then of that other seed sown in the dark underworld; and at last of the whole

Botticelli   *Photo Brogi*
THE CHILD WITH THE POMEGRANATE SURROUNDED BY ANGELS WITH LILIES AND ROSE-GARLANDS

(Uffizi Gallery, Florence)

[To face page 262

hidden region, which Dante visited. . . . Botticelli putting it into the childish hands of Him,
who, if men went down into hell, is there also.'

So, as the symbol of the life on the other side
of death, the pomegranate is exceedingly well
placed when given to the writer of the *Divina
Commedia*, and it is even more appropriate in
the hand of the incarnate Godhead—He who
holds our future destinies in the hollow of His
palm.

But it is difficult to ascertain if this was
really the thought in the minds of the Florentine
artists.

Mrs Jameson considers the pomegranate to
be the symbol of immortality, or, showing the
seeds, of hope in eternity.

But it would scarcely be the symbol of immortality in the Infant Saviour's hand, since the
symbol so placed is never His exclusive attribute,
but the indication of some relationship with
humanity. But showing the seeds—and the seeds
are usually shown—it might be the symbol of
a hope in eternity which He gives to man, the
parallel lying in the unexpected sweetness of
the fruit within the hard rind.

But possibly the authority followed by the masters of the 'Quattrocento,' or by those churchmen who gave them their commissions, was Gregory the Great, for he says: 'The pomegranate is the emblem of congregations because of its many seeds: also emblem of the Christian Church because of the inner unity of countless seeds in one and the same fruit.

Following this interpretation, the pomegranate, when carried by Dante or any other being of mortal birth, would indicate his faith in the Holy Catholic Church.

In Northern art the pomegranate is very rare. The Flemish artists ignore it, and those few German artists who paint it are those who had come under Italian influence. And it does not seem entirely clear whether those German artists who, like Hans Burgkmair,[1] paint it in the Infant Christ's hand, give to the Southern fruit the Southern significance, or if for them it becomes the fruit of Eden in the hand of the second Adam.

In scenes representing different events in the life of Christ, trees of pomegranates are

[1] German Museum, Nüremburg.

occasionally introduced. Giovanni di Paolo sets the ' Nativity '[1] in an orchard of pomegranates, and in a Florentine picture of the fourteenth century[2] the newly-risen Christ is surrounded by palms, pomegranates and flowers. These pomegranates, however, do not seem to be used attributively but merely to give some slight geographical indication. Bethlehem was an Eastern city; the tomb of Christ was in an Eastern garden.

The pomegranate is also, theoretically, the emblem of the Virgin. ' In the symbolism of the cult of Mary, the ripe pomegranate, because of its pleasant fragrance and its numerous seeds, represents her beauty and many virtues, but the gradually-developing fruit refers to her life.'[3]

' The pomegranate with its crowned top is her as queen, and typifies also hope and fruitfulness, the " Virginitas fecunda " of the octave of Christmas.'[4]

[1] Vatican Gallery.   [2] *Ibid.*
[3] Dr Anselm Salzer, O.S.B. *Die Sinnbilder und Beiworte Mariens in der deutschen Literatur und lateinischen Hymnenpoesie des Mittelalters.*
[4] Mrs Henry Jenner, *Christian Symbolism.*

Jeremy Taylor, in a beautiful passage, describes Mary as the pomegranate tree and Christ as the fruit.

' When the Holy Virgin now perceived that the expectation of the nations was arrived at the very doors of revelation and entrance into the world, she brought forth the *Holy Jesus*, who, like light through a transparent glass, past through, or a ripe pomegranate from a fruitful tree, fell to the earth, without doing violence to its nurse and parent.'

In art, however, the pomegranate is very seldom used as the attribute of the Virgin. Occasionally the Florentine masters ornament the Virgin's throne with knobs which more or less resemble the fruit, and Flemish artists, Memling in particular, place behind her a brocaded panel of the well-known pomegranate design. But these pomegranate knobs were a very usual detail in carved work, and the pomegranate pattern, which still persists, was a standard design of the silk-weavers of France and Italy.

The fruit itself is not used by the older masters. Even Crivelli, who lavishes fruit of almost every sort upon his slender, long-figured Madonnas, leaves the pomegranate aside.

In modern work, Podesti, in his vast fresco of the Immaculate Conception,[1] has placed a large single pomegranate upon a book arranged prominently in the foreground. It is the symbol, apparently, of the fruitfulness of the Virgin.

The ancient Jews ornamented their temple with the pomegranate, and their high priest's robes were bordered with alternate bells and pomegranates. In the Christian Church, too, they have been admitted as decoration, though not with any very clear and definite symbolical significance. There is a very handsome seventeenth-century altar-rail of marble on which rest candlesticks and huge brass pomegranates before the high altar in the ancient church of S. Cecilia in Rome; and a great bronze pomegranate, worn by much caressing, is on the balustrade in the tiny chapel which was once the bathroom of the saint.

[1] Vatican.

XXIII

THE STRAWBERRY

THE strawberry stands apart from all other symbolical fruits. It is found in Italian, Flemish and German art, and also in the English miniatures. There is a finely-executed Spanish miniature of the sixteenth century in South Kensington Museum. The Pelican in her Piety is in the centre and the border is formed of roses alternating with strawberries. As a symbol it is not only widespread, but of comparatively early origin. In Siena it appears as a flower of Heaven, growing with lilies, violets and carnations, in the 'Paradise' of Giovanni di Paolo painted in 1445;[1] and, almost at the same time, a master of the Upper Rhine painted the well-known 'Madonna of the Strawberries,'[2] which represents the Virgin sitting upon the edge of a

---

[1] Belle Arti, Siena.   [2] Town Museum, Solothurn.

raised bed filled with exquisitely-rendered strawberries.   Behind is a hedge of roses, and at her
feet violets and lilies of the valley.   In the foreground is a small figure of the donor kneeling
among tufts of snowdrops. The snowdrop is
rare as a symbol (though by no means misplaced
in a Madonna picture, having all the qualities,
except the perfume, of the lily of the valley),
and it was probably the individual fancy of
the donor.

The strawberry is not mentioned in Scripture,
neither does it seem to have been remarked by
those Fathers of the Church who concerned
themselves with symbolism, but it was very
successful in its appeal to the artists of the
Renaissance. It is a very perfect fruit, with
neither thorns nor stone, but sweet, soft and
delicious through and through. Its flowers
are of the whiteness of innocence and its leaves
almost of the sacred trefoil form, and since it
grows upon the ground, not on a tree, there is no
possibility of its being the dread fruit of the
Tree of Knowledge.

Its meaning always appears to be the same;
it is the symbol of perfect righteousness, or the

emblem of the righteous man whose fruits are good works.

As the symbol of perfect righteousness, in Italy it is chiefly used in 'Adorations,' where the Infant Christ is laid upon the ground among the grass. Botticelli seems to have been the first to have placed it among the violets and daisies, but he had many followers, and a very charming picture, with the little scarlet berries in the foreground, is the 'Adoration' by Perugino, now in Munich. Botticelli may, however, have borrowed the symbol from Giovanni di Paolo,[1] who painted a small minutely-finished picture of the Virgin, seated on a cushion, with the Holy Child in her arms. Behind are fruit trees and strawberries, violets and carnations are at her feet, and since it was usual in Siena, in pictures where the Infant Saviour appears, to refer all symbols to Him, they are His attributes. In German art of the fifteenth century, on the other hand, the symbolical plants, including the strawberry, which appears in

[1] Belle Arti, Siena.

the mystical 'Enclosed Gardens,' express the virtues of Mary.

The symbolical strawberry is almost invariably accompanied by the violet, from which we may gather that the truly fruitful soul is always humble.

XXIV

FRUIT IN GARLANDS

FRUIT in general signifies 'the fruits of the Spirit—joy, peace and love.' And therefore the painters of Northern Italy wove peach and plum, apples and grapes into heavy garlands, which they looped above the place where the Holy Child sat enthroned upon His mother's knee, or they laid fresh, ripe fruit upon the step where the Virgin's feet were resting.

The wreath of fruit, when festooned behind or below a saint, was more particularly a symbol of the good works of the righteous; when looped above his head, it is a festal wreath equalling the victor's crown. Such a wreath is that of mingled fruit and flowers above the head of Mantegna's 'Triumphant Saint George.' [1]

But the fruit in many of the devotional pictures of the earlier Venetian masters would

[1] Accademia, Venice.

seem, like the rose gardens of Florence, to be partly votive. They wished to give of their best, and the cool fruit which came in high-piled boats to the gardenless city among the lagoons seemed infinitely precious to them— more precious, for they were a practical race of traders, than the fragile blossoms of ephemeral flowers. Besides, except for pinks, which, judging from various pictures, grew then as now in pots along the balconies, flowers to serve as models were rare in Venice.

Garlands of fruit, excellently modelled but somewhat wanting in softness and bloom, are especially remarkable in the work of the pupils of Squarcione, who taught in Padua during the last half of the fifteenth century. This famous School of Art is known to have been well furnished with ancient marbles of Greek and Roman origin, and it is to be supposed that there the pupils acquired a love for the classical festooned wreath. Mantegna's wreaths, and those in the earlier work of Crivelli, are firmly bound and formal. But later, Crivelli laid classicism aside, painting fruit with a freedom and profusion which is quite his own, though

s

there is ever the feeling that it is sculptured and coloured stone, not soft and perfumed fruit-flesh. He, in one picture, paints fruit decoratively, bound with its foliage into a sort of bower for the Virgin, places it symbolically in the hand of the Infant Christ, and also lays it as a votive offering at the Virgin's feet.[1]

In a picture by Giorgio Schiavone, another pupil of Squarcione, odd little angels offer dishes of fruit to the Infant Christ.[2]

But, except in Northern Italy, fruit in garlands was more used in decoration than in devotional pictures. Magnificent wreaths of carved stone fruit and foliage droop on either side of the great circular windows of Siena Cathedral; there are heavy painted wreaths of it beneath the figures of the Apostles in the chapel of the Vatican decorated by Fra Angelico; and the Della Robbias enclosed some of their most lovely works, with apples, pears, lemons, pine-cones and pomegranates, growing stiffly and beautifully into a symmetrical border. Fruit-forms were, indeed, infinitely better suited

[1] Brera, Milan.   [2] National Gallery, London.

to the Della Robbia medium than were the
delicate petals of flowers.

The Florentines, too, often placed their
Madonnas in elaborate wooden frames of carved
and gilded fruit—remembering perhaps the
epithet of Saint Bernard, who styled the Virgin
Mary 'the sublime fruit of the earth,' [1] finding
in her the fulfilment of the prophecy:

'In that day shall the branch of the Lord
be beautiful and glorious, and the fruit of the
earth shall be excellent and comely.' [2]

But many of these garlands of fruit, or of
mixed fruit and flowers, are entirely decorative
with no hidden meaning. They were a very
usual festal decoration in the fourteenth and
fifteenth centuries, and when swung above the
head of Memling's 'Enthroned Madonna,' [3]
they are no more a symbol than is the carpet
beneath her feet, for an almost identical wreath,
held in place by the same small *putti*, is above
the throne in Gerard David's 'Judgment of
Cambyses,' [4] while one which is very similar

---

[1] Sermon on the Assumption of the Virgin.
[2] Isaiah iv. 2.   [3] Imperial Gallery, Vienna.
[4] Town Museum, Bruges.
  S *

hangs above the enthroned 'Emperor Sigis
mondo,'[1] incised upon the pavement of Siena
Cathedral. These wreaths distinguish the
throne as being more than an ordinary seat,
but, beyond vaguely indicating pomp and
splendour, they have no special meaning.

[1] Dom di Bartolo d'Asciano.

The Sacred Heart (19th Century—German)

THE PARADISE OF
GIOVANNI DI PAOLO

IN the Gallery of Siena there is a panel by Giovanni di Paola, the contemporary and occasional assistant of the better-known Sano di Pietro. The panel, which was painted in 1453, represents the Last Judgment, and, naturally, it is the portion of it which is given to Paradise, that is interesting because of its flower symbolism.

Heaven is depicted as a hill, for in the 15th century the prophet Esdras was the authority relied on for descriptions of the heavenly land, and Paradise, he says, has 'seven mighty mountains on which grow roses and lilies.' [1]

At the summit of the hill there are six fruit-bearing trees, for the prophet continues, 'Saith the Lord, ... I have sanctified and prepared for thee twelve trees laden with diverse fruit.'

There are six trees, not twelve, in this picture, for, by a convention common enough in early art, where the space did not admit of a certain number, that number was halved.

Beneath the trees wander the happy souls, of whom the greater part appear to have taken holy orders when in the flesh. Those just arrived are welcomed joyfully by the angels or by friends who had preceded them.

On the grassy bank there are lilies, the symbol of purity ; the carnation, equalling the rose as the flower of divine love, the violet of humility and the strawberry, whose fruit symbolises the good works of the righteous.

[1] II. Esdras II., 19.   II. Esdras II., 18.

277

These are the values of the flowers as symbols; as emblems they translate this Heaven as a perfected counter-part of the Church upon Earth, 'for' says Durandus, commenting on the text, 'See the smell of my son is as the smell of a field which the Lord hath blessed.' 'This field is the Church, which is verdant with flowers, which shineth with virtues, which is fragrant with good works; and wherein be the roses of martyrs, the lilies of virgins, the violets of confessors, and the verdure of beginners in the faith ' Following the same authority, the trees are emblems of righteous men, rich in good works. [1]

So for three different reasons the flowers in this painted Paradise appealed to the devout. They help to give a realistic picture of Heaven, presenting in form and colour the description of the prophet; they express mystically the Christian graces; they represent, to the instructed, the bands of martyrs, the choirs of virgins, and the countless happy souls for which the painter had no space.

The little childish beings, with wounds upon their necks or sides, are the Holy Innocents. Two climb up the lilies which are their attributes as virgin martyrs. Though unbaptised, the Innocents, since they died for Christ, were permitted to enter Heaven.

In the foreground, among the violets, are hares, the hare being an ancient emblem of a Christian, founded upon the words of Tertullian ' Upon us, as were we hares, is the hunt let loose.' [2]

Also the early naturalists averred that the hare slept with his eyes open; whence the prayer of Saint Mectilda:

'Grant, O Lord, that, like the hare, I may watch for Thee in Spirit, even while my body takes its needful repose. [3]

Rat. Off. of. Altars.   [2] Ad. Nat., 2, 3.
[3] Spiritual Grace.

Giovanni di Paolo

PARADISE

(Instituto delle Belle Arti, Siena)

Photo Brogi

To face page 278

THE QUEEN OF HEAVEN

BY

HUBERT van EYKE

O N the 6th of May, 1432, the great altar-piece painted by Hubert and Jan van Eyke, entitled 'The Adoration of the Mystic Lamb,' was erected as a finished work in the Church of S. Bavon in Ghent.

Each of its twelve panels is extremely interesting but the detail which is most important in connection with flower symbolism is the crown of the Madonna. Mary as Queen of Heaven, is seated on the right hand of God the Father, her head is slightly bowed as she reads from the book which she holds open.

Her crown is of gold, set with pearls, sapphires and rubies. Above each large square-cut ruby is placed a lily with two dark-blue columbines at its base. Above the sapphires and alternate with the lilies, are roses, each surmounted by three slender stalks of lily of the valley. A cluster of diaphanous gold stars form a sort of aureole.

The symbolism of jewels is complicated and confused, varying with different authorities, but that of flowers is almost always unchanged. In this crown the *lilium candidum*, which takes the place of the golden fleurs-de-lys that ornament the crowns of earthly queens, indicates the purity of body and of soul by which the Virgin had found favour in God's sight. The roses, three in number, denote the Divine Love of the Holy Trinity, and since these are placed, though singly, in a crown, they hold also some measure of heavenly joy.

The seven blooms of the columbine, symbolize the seven gifts of the Holy Spirit, which, when attributed to the Virgin, are, Faith, Hope, Charity, Justice, Prudence, Temperance, and Strength.

The lily of the valley, found only in northern symbolism, typifies the meekness and 'low estate' of the 'hand-maid of the Lord.'

The twelve stars suggested by the starry crown of the Apocalypse, are said by some authorities to represent the twelve Apostles, illustrating Mary's title of 'Regina Apostolorum.' The 'great wonder' had appeared in Heaven and the lily-like maid was now a queen, 'the woman clothed with the sun, and upon her head a crown of twelve stars.'

Hubert van Eyke

THE QUEEN OF HEAVEN
(From copy by Coxie, Alte Pinakothek, Munich)

[To face page 280

THE ADORATION
OF THE SHEPHERDS

BY

HUGO VAN DER GOES.

THERE has been lately placed in the Uffizi Gallery, the large 'Adoration of the Shepherds,' by Hugo van der Goes, which was painted between 1470 and 1475 by order of Tommaso Portinari, agent of the Medici in Bruges, for the Chapel of the Florentine Hospital of Santa Maria Nuova.

It is a tryptich. On the side wings are the donor and his family ; in the centre is the 'Adoration of the Shepherds.'

Upon the ground in the courtyard of a stable, the Holy Child lies in a pool of light emanating from Himself. His mother kneels beside Him, and plain little angels with jewelled head-dresses form a circle round them. To the right is a group of adoring shepherds—to the left Saint Joseph.

In the foreground of the picture, before the Infant Christ, there lies a sheaf of corn. There are also two vases. One is of pottery, with a conventional design of grapes and vine leaves, and is filled with orange lilies and the purple and the white iris. In the other, which is of transparent glass, there is columbine and three red carnations ; upon the ground are scattered blue and white violets. Each flower is painted with the most exquisite precision. Here the flower symbols all emphasize the spiritual significance of the scene. The scattered violets symbolize humility, for the King of Heaven lies on the ground as a little Child. The white ones among them may denote the innocence of His babyhood. The transparent glass so often seen in Annunciations, is the symbol of His immaculate conception, the group of carnations, alike in shape and colour, typifies the divine love of the triune Godhead, which moved the Son to take a human form for our salvation. The seven blossoms of the columbine, the flower of the dove, are symbols of the seven gifts of the Holy Spirit with which He was endowed at birth. The lilies in the vase are His own emblem as the King of Heaven, since He said: 'I am the flower of the field, and the lily of the valleys.' They are not the *lilium candidum*, the flower of the Madonna's purity, but the royal lilies of the field, orange, purple and white. Even Solomon, in gold, purple and fine linen, 'was not arrayed like one of these.'

Lastly there is the vine, pictured upon the vase, and the sheaf of corn, the eucharistic substances which in the sacrifice of the Mass, repeat the sacrifice for which He was born into the world as a little child.

It has been said, and reproachfully, of the Northern artists that they preferred gold, jewels and rich embroideries to the more ephemeral loveliness of flowers. This dictum may be just when applied to the early German schools; of Flemish Art it is not true. In this picture, for instance, the little angels are richly dressed but not rose-crowned like their Florentine cousins. They wear instead circlets of precious stones and pearls, from which spring aigrettes with pendant jewels. They carry no flowers and no flowers are used to fill vacant spaces in the picture. Flowers are reserved instead for the highest use of all and are placed in the forefront of the scene to represent the virtues of the Holy One.

Hugo van der Goes has painted almost these same flowers of the Adoration in his Fall.[1] Adam and Eve stand beneath the tree from which Eve reaches an apple. The lizard-bodied tempter stands behind. In the centre of the foreground, in front of the figures, is the iris, the columbine, the violet, a rose-bush not yet in bloom and the strawberry. There is also a pansy (which is rare as a symbol, except in England where it was named Herb Trinity,) and its meaning in this picture does not seem clear.

These flowers, used elsewhere as the emblems and attributes of Jesus Christ, here are introduced to recall the coming of the 'second Adam,' exactly reversing the symbolism which places an apple in the hand of the Infant Christ.

---

[1] Imperial Gallery, Vienna.

Hugo van der Goes   *Photo Brogi*

THE ADORATION OF THE SHEPHERDS
(Uffizi Gallery, Florence)

To face page 282

THE IMMACULATE
CONCEPTION

MURILLO

I N the 17th century the Spanish Inquisition appointed certain *familiares* whose warrant ran :

'We give him commission and charge him hence forward that he take particular care to inspect and visit all paintings of sacred subjects which may stand in shops or in public places ; if he finds anything to object to in them he is to take the picture before the Lords of the Inquisition.'

Murillo, painting for the Church in Seville, the most orthodox city of Spain, may therefore be reckoned correct in his method of presenting sacred subjects. At the period in which he painted, the particular form of Madonna picture most often ordered by the Spanish Church, was that known as the 'Immaculate Conception.'

The sinless birth of the Virgin was a dogma that had been adopted enthusiastically by the Spanish, so much so that Philip III and Philip IV sent special embassies to Rome to obtain more explicit papal recognition of the doctrine. It did not, however, become an article of of faith till 1854 and, as a subject, it is chiefly confined to the Spanish School.

The scheme of the picture is invariably taken from the Revelation of St. John.

'And there appeared a great wonder in Heaven ; a woman clothed with the sun, and the moon under her feet, and upon her head a crown of twelve stars '

It was usual to add a group of *putti* about the Virgin's feet (her feet, according to an injunction of the Inquisition as to 'decency' being carefully covered) and these *putti* almost always carried flowers, the rose, lily, olive and palm. Sometimes the iris was added, and occasionally the iris alone was used.[1] Very often a *putto* carries a looking-glass,[2] a symbol of the Immaculate Conception which appears to be of Spanish origin, but which is perhaps a variation or development of the transparent vase, which in the 15th century art was a symbol of the virgin birth of Christ. The idea is that the glass, whatever be the image cast upon it, remains in itself unstained.

In Murillo's masterpiece, '*La Purissima*' of the Prado, the flowers indicate Mary's virtues. The rose, symbol of love and mercy, show her as the *Mater misericordiæ;* the lily shows her purity—she is '*La Purissima:*' the palm of triumph is hers as the Queen of Heaven and the olive tells of the healing she brings to mankind; she is the *Consolatrix Afflictorum.*

And the Church having identified the Virgin with the 'Wisdom' of the 24th Chapter of Ecclesiasticus, these symbols are also her direct emblems, for, says Wisdom:

'I was exalted like a palm-tree in Engaddi, and as a rose-plant in Jericho, as a fair olive-tree in a pleasant field.'

And the lily is always her emblem as 'The lily of the valleys.'

It is noticeable that this figure of the Virgin, realized from the word picture of the Revelation of Saint John, was one that appealed strongly to the Spanish. She is 'clothed with the sun and the moon under her feet.' The moon is represented as the crescent moon which was the sacred device of the followers of Mahomet, and which had surmounted innumerable mosques throughout the Iberian peninsula for more than five hundred years. Ferdinand, husband of Isabella, put an end to the Moorish dominion in 1492, but the impress of the Moor is to this day strong on the land, and in the 17th century it seemed a fitting thing that the Virgin's foot should be upon the hated crescent which symbolized Moorish rule and the faith of Islam. It was therefore, as a symbol of the Mohamedan faith [rather than as a symbol of chastity through its connection with the Goddess Diana, as is sometimes suggested], that representations of the Virgin with her feet upon a crescent, became so popular in Spain.

[1] José Antolines, Alte Pinakothek, Munich.　　[2] Murillo, Prado, Madrid.

Murillo   Photo Anderson

THE IMMACULATE CONCEPTION
(Prado, Madrid)

To face page 284

THE GIRLHOOD OF
MARY VIRGIN

DANTE GABRIEL ROSSETTI

IN the year 1848, three young English painters, Dante Gabriel
Rossetti, John Everett Millais and William Holman Hunt, founded
the Preraphaelite Brotherhood, the aim of which was to bring back
to modern art the sincerity of those painters who had preceded Raphael.

The original characteristics of the brotherhood's work were a
simplicity in the types chosen and a workmanship almost Flemish in
its careful and minute finish. But later, and more particularly in the
work of Rossetti, 'Preraphaelism' became associated with a certain
mysticism of subject whose deeper meaning was accentuated and
elucidated by the use of symbols and more especially flower symbols.

Rossetti's earliest exhibited work was 'The Girlhood of Mary Virgin,'
painted in 1849.

The Virgin with Saint Anne by her side, sits at an embroidery
frame and works upon a strip of red material the lily with two flowers
and a bud which grows in a vase before her. A little rosy winged angel
waters the lily, and, lying crossed upon the ground, is a seven-leaved
palm and a seven-thorned briar, united by a little scroll bearing the
words '*Tot dolores, tot gaudia.*'

The second part of the double sonnet written by the artist for this
picture explains to some extent the symbolism.

II

These are the symbols.   On that cloth of red
I' the centre is the Tripoint : perfect each
Except the second of its points, to teach
That Christ is not yet born.   The books—whose head
Is golden charity, as Paul hath said—
Those virtues are wherein the soul is rich :
Therefore on them the lily standeth, which
Is innocence, being interpreted.

The seven-thorn'd briar and the palm seven-leaved,
Are her great sorrow and her great reward.
Until the end be full, the Holy One
Abides without.   She soon shall have achieved
Her perfect purity : yea, God the Lord
Shall soon vouchsafe His Son to be her Son.

Behind the Virgin is the trellis of the ' Enclosed Garden.' Beyond—
for still the ' Holy One abides without '—is the vine, emblem of the
' True Vine,' the figure of Saint Joseph, who tends it, forecasting that
he would be the guardian of Christ's infancy.   Upon the trellis, up
which wreathes the white convolvulus, used in the 15th century as the
symbol of humility, sits the Holy Dove.

Finally, upon the balustrade is a rose in a transparent vase, the rose
of divine love conjoined with the symbol of transcendant purity.

Dante Gabriel Rossetti   Photo Mansell

THE GIRLHOOD OF MARY VIRGIN

To face page 280

LIST OF AUTHORITIES

Antony, Joseph, *Symbolik der Katholischen Kirchen Gebrauche*

Archæologia

Augustine, St, *Confessions*

Beaumont, de, *Recherches sur l'origine du Blazon et en particulier la Fleur-de-Lis*

Bernard of Clairvaux, St, *Sermons*

Biblia Pauperum, Heidelberg Copy, 1440; German Ed., 1471, Wolfenbüttel Copy

Byzantine Guide to Painting (Didron's Translation)

Dante, *Divina Commedia*

Didron, *Christian Iconography*

Durandus, *Rational of the Divine Offices*

Edmonson, *Complete Book of Heraldry*, 1780

Ford, *Spanish Handbook* (First Edition)

Hirn, Yrjö, *The Sacred Shrine*

Huysman, J. K., *La Cathédrale*

Jacobus de Voragine, *Legenda Aurea*

Jameson, Mrs, *Sacred and Legendary Art*

Jenner, Mrs H., *Christian Symbolism*

Liebman, P. S., *Kleine Handwörterbuch der Christlichen Symbolik*

Martin, Arthur, *Mélanges d'Archéologie*

Mectilda, St, *Spiritual Grace*

Menzel, Wolfgang, *Christliche Symbolik*

287

Neale, J. M., *Hymni Ecclesiae*

Northcote and Brownlow, *Roma Sotterana*

Schmid, A., *Christliche Symbole aus alter und neuer Zeit*

Smith, *Classical Dictionary*

Strabo, Walafrid, *Hortulus*

Syrian Codice of 586, Laurentian Library

Taylor, Jeremy, *The History of the Life and Death of the Holy Jesus*

Tertullian

Twining, Louisa, *Symbols and Emblems*

Vasari, *Lives of the Painters*

Venturi, *Storia dell' Arte Italiana*

INDEX OF ARTISTS

289

INDEX OF FLOWERS

291

THE CHILDHOOD OF ART; or, The Ascent

of **Man.** A Sketch of the Vicissitudes of his Upward Struggle, based chiefly on the Relics of his Artistic Work in Prehistoric Times. By H. G. SPEARING, M.A., Queen's College, Oxford. With 16 Plates in Colour and nearly 500 Illustrations in Black and White. Royal 8vo, **21/-** net.

BIBLE WAYS IN BIBLE LANDS: An

Impression of Palestine. By MAUDE M. HOLBACH, author of ''Dalmatia, the Land where East meets West.'' With Thirty-two beautiful Illustrations from Photographs taken by Otto Holbach. Crown 8vo, **5/-** net.

This interesting volume records the author's impressions of the Holy Land. She shows the unchangingness of the East, sketching for those who cannot visit Bible Lands the landscapes and the people, and describes the customs of everyday life that our Master drew upon to illustrate His spiritual teachings as they are to-day—that is, almost exactly as they were nineteen hundred years ago. The book makes a strong appeal to Bible students.

FRANCIA'S MASTERPIECE: An Essay on

the Beginnings of the Immaculate Conception in Art. By MONTGOMERY CARMICHAEL, author of '' In Tuscany,'' etc. With 10 Plates. Crown 8vo, **5/-** net.

THE FLORA OF THE SACRED NATIVITY:

An Attempt at collecting the Legends and Ancient Dedications of Plants connected in Popular Tradition with the Life of Our Blessed Lord from His Nativity to the Flight into Egypt. By ALFRED E. P. RAYMUND DOWLING, B.A., St John's College, Oxford. Demy 8vo, **7/6** net.

LEGENDS OF OUR LORD AND THE HOLY

FAMILY. By Mrs ARTHUR BELL. With 32 Illustrations from the Old Masters. Crown 8vo, **6/-** net.

KEGAN PAUL, TRENCH, TRÜBNER & CO. Limited

CPSIA information can be obtained
at www.ICGtesting.com
Printed in the USA
LVHW090907191120
672055LV00024B/621